TOP 7 STRATEGIC TRENDS FOR SOCIAL MEDIA MARKETING IN 2024

From Leveraging AI to Dominating Social Commerce, Learning the Latest Trends and Techniques for Success Online

George I. Spears

All rights reserved. No part of this publication maybe reproduced, distributed, or transmitted in any form or by all means, including photocopying, recording, or other electronic or mechanical methods, without the prior written permission of the publisher, except in case of belief quotations embodied in critical reviews and certain other noncommercial uses permitted by copyright law

Copyright © (George I. Spears), (2024).

Table of contents

Introduction...6
    marketing on social media, What is it?.....................7
    Benefits of Social Media Marketing.......................... 8
    7 Chic Social Media Marketing Locations for Businesses.. 10
    Important Rudiments of a Winning Social Media Marketing Plan.. 13

Trend 1: AI-Powered Personalization....................... 17
    How To Use AI for Social Media Marketing in 2024 18
    Anticipatory Analytics for ROI in Social Media........23
    How to implement AI-powered personalization?.... 26
    Benefits of AI-driven customization....................... 28
    Examples and Case Studies...................................29
    Case Studies.. 38

Trend 2: Augmented Reality (AR) Experiences....... 40
    How to Use AR in Your Social Media Marketing Plan for 2024..42
    Instances of Effective AR Campaigns in 2024........45
    Strategies for Implementing Augmented Reality in Social Media Marketing.. 53
    How to Lead an Effective Augmented Reality Implementation?... 54
    Case Study and Examples....................................... 58

Trend 3: Video Content Dominance........................ 60
    The Impact of Social Media Platforms.................... 65

Handling the Difficulties of Going Viral..................76
Using Videotape Content to Its Fullest Implicit for Marketing Success..................79
Creating Your 2024 Social Media Objective..........81
The Significance of thickness in Social Media........82
Practical Advice for Upholding Social Media Regularity..................82
Innovative styles and Stylish Practices..................84
a visual calendar-style overview of your social media content strategy.....................88

Trend 4: Influencer Collaboration Evolution............91
Influencer marketing: what is it?..................91
Important components that characterize influencer marketing:..................93
The Transformation of Social Media Influencer Marketing..................94
Innovative Techniques for Working with Influencers...100
Forming Alliances That Will Benefit Both Parties. 103
Utilizing Various Influencer Types........................104
Working together with Nano and Micro Influencers....105

Trend 5: Engagement and Community Building... 108
The Value of Creating Virtual Communities..........110
Strategies for Creating Communities in 2024....... 114
User-Generated Content and Advocacy within Communities..................126
The Influence of Community Development and Authenticity..................128
The Profit-Return Explosion: Making Gold Out of

User Content..130
   Brands Mastering the UGC Game: Exemplary Case Studies...131
   Best Practices to Remember...............................134
Trend 6: Ephemeral Content and Storytelling....... 136
   Social media content types that are transient.......138
   Telling Stories to Engage People with Your Brand..... 140
   Why brands may benefit from ephemeral content 152
   How Your Marketing Strategy Can Include Ephemeral Content..159
Trend 7: Social Commerce.. 163
   The rise of social media platforms for commerce. 165
   Market volume and forecasts................................166
   Recognizing the Effects of Social Media on E-Commerce..168
   Integrating social networks and e-commerce platforms is the evolution of shopping..................171
   The advantages of social commerce....................174
   Implementing Effective Social Commerce Strategies: 178
   3 Top Social Media Ecommerce Tools for 2024....183
Conclusion.. 186

Introduction

Professionals in social media marketing have observed significant shifts in the way people use social media platforms and the kinds of content that are posted there. Because Tiktok's popularity demonstrated that short videotape content is the solution to the fashionability of today's youth, Instagram jumped on the Tiktok ban in several areas and made its rolls even more popular.

Facebook introduced Watch Party and other videotape content, following suit with the rest of the industry. The number of social media addicts worldwide is expected to reach nearly 5 billion by 2024, and as AI and ML take over the Internet, the social media landscape will undergo significant transformations.

Social media marketers frequently observe that they have prepared themselves for 2024 by creating more captivating and alluring content to entice drug users of all stripes and age groups. Despite this, the followership exertion on social media platforms has drastically changed as a result of the ongoing refinement in the taste and type of content. If you want to continue offering your goods and services online in 2024, you will still need to adopt digital marketing techniques and social media trends that will enable you to draw in new business from implicit prospects while also retaining the loyalty of current patrons.

These days, social media marketing plays a major role in the marketing strategies of both big and small businesses. Given that there are 4.9 billion drug users on social media, having a presence there is an excellent way to converse with both current and potential customers. Regardless of your industry, social media is a crucial tool for reaching your target audience, building brand equity, attracting loyal customers, and closing more sales. In this book, we go over all the important details about social media marketing, such as its definition, trends, and chic techniques.

marketing on social media, What is it?

The practice of using social media platforms—where people create social networks and exchange information—to improve a business's online visibility, close deals, and improve website traffic is known as social media marketing, sometimes known as digital marketing or e-marketing. SMM offers businesses a way to communicate with their existing customers and draw in new ones, as well as built-in data analytics tools that allow marketers to assess the efficacy of their juggernauts and identify fresh opportunities for engagement.

The success of a social media marketing campaign depends on strategy and planning. Once you've written your business biographies, you'll need to update and improve them. The next step is to create a content schedule that specifies the content you will publish, where you will publish it, and when. It is likely that your bulletins will incorporate stories, videos, prints, and textbooks to tell an engaging tale, highlight your company, and attract the proper kind of audience.

In order to maintain your integrity and flawlessly build a community, you'll respond to criticism, likes, and shares in addition to creating fresh, regular content. Depending on your budget and specific goals, paid social media ads may also be a part of your plan. These ads use social media marketing to show your company to the appropriate audiences at the appropriate times.

Benefits of Social Media Marketing

Due to its widespread usage and inflexibility, social media is a useful tool for creating commercial content. It's also genuinely measurable in contrast to other traditional marketing techniques like print ads, radio commercials, and billboards. Some of the most noteworthy benefits of social media marketing are listed below.

Add a Mortal Touch to Your Enterprise Through social media platforms, you can interact with both explicit and implicit guests. If you use them wisely, you can "humanize your brand" and build a closer relationship with your followers. Encourage Traffic By including links to your website in all of your social media bulletins, you can potentially increase applicable business to your website. This type of business has the ability to improve your hunt machine optimization and convert callers into customers. SEO, or search engine optimization, is yet another crucial business expansion tactic. Learn more about SEO and the best SEO firms.

Generate Leads With social media tools like call-to-action buttons, Facebook and Instagram shops, and direct messaging, you can generate leads and conversions. Increasing leads and conversions is an effective way to increase sales. Increase brand awareness For small and new businesses, social media marketing is a fantastic way to present their brands. You can use it to make it clearer how you differ from your competitors and, ideally, perform better. Make ties You must build relationships with your customers if you hope to retain them over time.

Social media makes it easy to communicate with your followers, which makes it a useful tool for building connections.

7 Chic Social Media Marketing Locations for Businesses

There are a number of social media marketing platforms that you might want to use when developing a social plan. As you weigh your options, you'll find that certain platforms are better suited for your target request and brand than others. This is a concise overview of numerous platforms that could assist you in optimizing your social media marketing efforts.

1. Facebook
As Facebook is the most widely used social media platform, using it can benefit almost any kind of business. It can be applied to increase sales, generate leads, gain followers, and improve brand visibility. It also offers a chance to display announcements that are targeted and highly customizable. Recall that there is fierce competition on Facebook despite its importance as a tool for social media marketing.

2. WhatsApp
Originally, Instagram was just a print-participating website. Over time, it has evolved into a situation where businesses can engage with their followership through visually striking photos and videos. Moreover, Instagram features stores, rolls, live streaming, shops, and stories that can help you make the most of your campaign. Instagram is a fantastic choice if your business sells its products or services through images.

3. Using X (former Twitter)
"Tweets" on X are short postings that include text, photographs, videos, animated GIFs, and links. X can help you engage your audience with concise but insightful messaging. Depending on your type of business, it may allow you to search for information and topics about your target market and industry, provide customer support, and raise brand

awareness. A tweet typically has a maximum length of 280 characters.

4. You Tube
After Google, YouTube is the second-biggest search engine and a social media streaming network. If your company is willing and able to create quality video content, you should absolutely be keeping an eye on YouTube. You may do a lot of things with YouTube, such highlight intriguing procedures, break down difficult subjects, highlight the special qualities of your products, and much more. It's a fantastic method to incorporate videos into your advertising plan.

5. The Pinterest
Users are inspired by Pinterest, which is referred to as a "visual discovery engine." Users frequently look via the platform for inspiration to help them design weddings, remodel their houses, go on idyllic trips, and accomplish other life goals. Pinterest is the best place to start if your business offers goods or services that help people find and realize their goals.

6. LinkedIn
For business-to-business (B2B) networking, LinkedIn is an especially helpful medium. It's intended for experts and can help you share your knowledge of the field. Additionally, you might

utilize it to engage with your staff, advertise job openings inside your organization, and even create leads through paid advertisements.

7. The TikTok
Short-form videos are the main focus of the more recent social media network TikTok. If you're attempting to attract a specific demographic, it might make sense because it tends to target younger girls. You can utilize hashtags related to your content, brand, and offerings on TikTok as a business. Users may find your content when they search for these hashtags.

Important Rudiments of a Winning Social Media Marketing Plan

While it might be tempting to post anything on many social networking spots whenever you feel like it, this isn't recommended. To maximize the benefits of social media marketing and increase the liability of success, you need a solid social media plan.

In short, a social media strategy is a plan that specifies your pretensions on social media, the way you will take to achieve them, and the KPIs you will track. These are the abecedarian factors of an effective social media strategy.

followership exploration previous to publishing anything, you should have a solid understanding of your target followership. Answer inquiries about the platforms they use, the content types they prefer, and the other druggies they follow.

Brand Identity Decide how you want to interact with your followers and post on social media to represent your business. suppose about the arguments you wish to present.

Your plan for using content on social media platforms to grow your brand and addict base is known as your content strategy. The more specific your plan is, the more likely it's to succeed.

Analytics Social media analytics is the process of collecting and assaying data from your social media accounts in order to estimate performance and modify your strategy. Without it, you will not be suitable to assess the success of your sweats.

Constant Action Social media marketing is a constant process, much like the maturity of marketing strategies. It's necessary to post constantly, communicate with your followers, and optimize your profile.

Social media marketing experts have noticed notable changes in the content participated on social media platforms and how druggies interact with them. With its own rolls, Instagram jumped on the crusade, staking on Tiktok's original ban and growing in fashionability. The fashionability of Tiktok demonstrated that the result of the appeal of the current generation is short videotape content. In line with the trend, Facebook debuted Watch Party and other videotape content.

There are presently 5 billion social media druggies encyclopedia ally, and that number is rising at a now - ahead - seen rate. The Internet will be dominated by AI and ML by 2024, drastically altering the social media scene.

Since followership exertion on social media platforms has drastically changed due to the constant elaboration of content taste and type, it's common to observe that social media marketers have braced themselves for 2024 with further witching
and charming content to allure druggies of all kinds and age groups.

You'll need to use digital marketing strategies and social media trends in 2024 if you want to keep dealing with your products and services online. These strategies will help you draw in new guests while keeping your living bones pious.

This companion to social media marketing trends will bandy the newest products available and what you should be doing in 2024 and further.

The main reason for the changes in social media marketing strategy until a many times ago was the preface of new features and content motifs. still, due to shifts in work schedules, lockdowns, and working from home programs, followership geste

These are the top 7 social media and digital marketing trends that can help your business succeed in Machiavellian requests.

Trend 1: AI-Powered Personalization

With the world going more digital, companies are coming up with new strategies to interact with guests and give them a more customized experience. The use of machine literacy and artificial intelligence(AI) to produce personalized consumer gests is an intriguing development in this field. Massive volumes of consumer data, ranging from browsing and purchase histories to social media relations and demographic data, are gathered and anatomized for AI- powered customization.

The purpose of this data is to understand the unique conditions and preferences of every single consumer. Amazon's recommendation machine is a well- known illustration of AI- powered personalization in action.

The system predicts products the stoner would be interested in and makes real- time recommendations for them by using a machine learning algorithm to examine hunt histories, purchase histories, and other behavioral data. Deals and consumer engagement for Amazon have increased significantly as a result of these customized recommendations.

How To Use AI for Social Media Marketing in 2024

Artificial Intelligence(AI) has been a game- changer in a number of diligence lately, changing the way enterprises run. Marketing on social media isn't an exception. AI is becoming a vital tool for marketers to ameliorate their social media strategy because of the vast quantum of data that's available and the demand for personalized guests .

This book will examine the colorful operations of AI in social media marketing in 2024, which will transfigure the way businesses interact with their target request. Artificial Intelligence- powered Content product A primary handicap encountered by social media marketers is the regular creation of witching and material content. AI technologies have a big part to play in working this problem. In 2024, marketers are able to save a significant quantum of time and trouble by using AI- powered content creation tools to automatically induce engaging social media posts.

Large volumes of data can be anatomized by tools like Natural Language Processing (NLP) algorithms to determine sentiments, client preferences, and current trends. Through the application of this technology, marketers can produce customized content that strikes a passion with their intended followership, leading to enhanced situations of engagement and conversion rates. AI- powered content product tools can also propel machine optimization, guaranteeing that a larger followership will see the brand's communication.

AI algorithms have the capacity to ameliorate social media post-exposure through the strategic use of keywords and content structuring, hence performing in heightened organic reach and website business. Increased Interaction with guests By 2024, advances in AI'll open the door to further engaging guests on social media. Natural Language Understanding (NLU) and sentiment analysis- enabled chatbots will advance in complication and be suitable to respond to consumer inquiries in real- time and with personalization.

With the help of these AI chatbots, brands will be suitable to give prompt help and support, perfecting the consumer experience. Handling several client relations at formerly will simplify client service procedures and free up staff members for more delicate jobs. also, marketers will be suitable to track social media conversations and determine public comprehension of their goods and services thanks to AI- driven sentiment analysis. This perceptive information can help marketers in modifying their tactics, attending to consumer issues, and spotting new trends, all of which will enhance client happiness and brand perception. Better Spotting Algorithms driven by AI have the eventuality to give social media advertisers a wealth of information on the tastes and geste of their followership.

AI can induce extremely accurate customer biographies, which expedites the targeting process, by assessing massive volumes of behavioral, psychographic, and demographic data. By 2024, artificial intelligence will be used more and more to pinpoint implicit consumers and ameliorate announcement targeting. Marketers may determine which target parts are most applicable for their advertisements by using AI's prophetic chops, which will ameliorate conversion rates and return on advertising spend(ROAS).

Individualized content delivery to individual druggies depending on their tastes and habits will also be eased by AI- driven results. Artificial intelligence(AI) algorithms can identify the stylish content to feature by examining druggies' former relations and engagement habits. This helps to make a stronger relationship between brands and their target followership. assaying Sentiment and Social harkening Sustaining a positive brand character requires keeping an eye on brand mentions on social media and comprehending consumer opinion.

In 2024, social listening and sentiment analysis ways driven by Al have advanced to the point that marketers can gain over- to- date information on customer preferences, opinions, and trends. Massive volumes of social media data are anatomized by AI algorithms, which also discover arising themes or enterprises that are material to the brand and track changes in sentiment.

With the use of this perceptive data, marketers can optimize the results of their social media juggernauts, proactively address issues, and make crusade adaptations. Brands can continuously assess public sentiment toward their products or services by exercising AI- powered sentiment analysis results.

Marketers may also use this information to target their messaging, manage their character proactively, and subsidize on favorable opinion to increase brand mindfulness.

Influencer Promotion

Influencer marketing has grown in popularity as a means for firms to establish a genuine connection with their target demographic. By 2024, influencer marketing campaigns will be significantly improved by artificial intelligence.

AI-powered technologies are able to examine the brand relevancy, engagement rates, and demographics of influencer audiences. Marketers may choose the most impactful influencers to work with and maximize conversions by using AI algorithms to choose influencers.

AI can also improve influencer marketing campaign tracking and measurement. Influencer post performance data, including sentiment, reach, engagement, and conversions, can be analyzed by AI algorithms. Marketers can make well-informed decisions, optimize their tactics, and guarantee a higher return on investment from their influencer collaborations by utilizing this data-driven method.

Improved Analysis of Competition

Artificial intelligence (AI)-powered social listening platforms will give marketers sophisticated competitive intelligence in addition to sentiment analysis and brand mention monitoring. AI algorithms will be able to monitor and examine rivals' social media platform activity in 2024, giving important information about their tactics, content, and audience interaction.

Marketers can learn more about the advantages and disadvantages of their rivals by using AI-driven competitive analysis solutions. They may utilize this data to improve their own social media marketing tactics, spot market gaps, and set their company out in a crowded field.

Additionally, marketers can have a comprehensive understanding of the social media environment by using AI to evaluate data from various social media platforms and channels. Artificial intelligence (AI) algorithms can detect new trends, industry influencers, and possible collaboration opportunities by combining data from several sources. This can improve the overall efficacy of social media marketing initiatives.

Anticipatory Analytics for ROI in Social Media

For marketers, calculating the return on investment (ROI) of social media marketing has never been easy. Predictive analytics technologies driven by AI will make ROI measurement more precise and trustworthy by 2024.

Artificial intelligence (AI) algorithms can forecast the results of social media marketing initiatives by examining past data and seeing trends. Marketers can use this predictive power to make data-driven decisions, enhance their strategies, and allocate funds wisely.

Predictive analytics driven by AI can also reveal information about consumer behavior and buy intent. Marketers can estimate conversion rates, identify potential prospects, and adjust their messaging by examining social media interactions and engagement trends.

Social media advertising that is automated

In 2024, Artificial intelligence is vital for automating and improving social media advertising operations.. In order to maximize the impact of advertising efforts, AI algorithms may evaluate enormous data sets to identify high-performing ad styles, target audiences, and bidding methods.

Ad campaign settings can be continuously monitored and adjusted in real-time by AI-powered automated bidding and optimization technologies, ensuring that the ad spend is distributed to the most productive channels and audience segments. Higher total ROAS, lower expenses, and better ad performance are the results of this dynamic optimization.

AI can help optimize ad creativity by examining past performance data and consumer preferences. Marketers may create customized ad variations and test them in real-time by utilizing AI algorithms. This allows them to determine which headlines, calls-to-action, and images are the most captivating and effective.

Visual Recognition for Intelligent Social Media Listening
Images become ever more important in brand communication as social media platforms develop. By 2024, social media listening skills will be improved by AI-driven image identification technologies, enabling marketers to assess and comprehend the influence of visual material on their brand.

AI systems are able to recognize company logos, merchandise, and visual mentions by analyzing photos and videos from various social media networks. With the aid of image recognition technology, marketers can track brand visibility, evaluate the overall effect of their visual communication campaigns, and learn more about user-generated content.

Visual recognition can also be used to find brand advocates or influencers who produce and distribute brand-related material. Marketers can interact with influential individuals and increase brand reach by using this data in influencer marketing initiatives.

How to implement AI-powered personalization?

Careful preparation and execution are necessary when using AI to create a successful personalization strategy. The following are some helpful pointers for creating a personalized AI-powered system:

Establish goals: Prior to putting into practice an AI-powered personalization, it is important to understand why personalization is necessary in the first place. For instance, a company can need customisation to boost sales, enhance client happiness, lower attrition, etc. The formulation and implementation of a strategy to accomplish underlying objectives must be guided by the clarity of personalized objectives.

Make use of high-quality data: The quality and volume of the customer data that is currently available have a significant impact on how effective AI-powered personalization is. Companies should create a system for gathering and archiving high-quality data so they may use it to understand the preferences and behavior of their customers.

Test and improve: In order to maintain the customization strategy current and improved based on user input, it should be regularly tested and improved.

Be open: You should be open about how you acquire and use client data for personalization in order to gain their trust. This entails outlining precise privacy guidelines and describing the ways in which client data is utilized to provide tailored experiences.

Customize across channels: Email, social media, in-store interactions, and other customer touchpoints should all incorporate personalization. This guarantees a consistent and customized client experience over all channels.

Benefits of AI-driven customization

Personalization enabled by AI has several benefits for enterprises. The following are a few of the strongest benefits:

Better customer experience: AI-powered personalization may greatly increase customer happiness and loyalty by customizing the customer experience to each individual's preferences and demands. Customers feel valued and understood when they receive a personalized experience, and this could lead to more interaction.

Increased income: Businesses can raise the possibility of a sale and increase total revenue by recommending goods and deals that are extremely relevant to each particular customer.

Decreased customer attrition: AI-driven personalization can assist lower attrition rates by offering tailored experiences that cater to individual customers' demands. Consumers are more likely to stick with a company that knows them and gives them a tailored experience.

Data-driven insights: AI-driven customisation offers insightful information about the habits and preferences of every client. By using this data, businesses may gain a deeper understanding of their clientele and tailor their marketing and sales tactics accordingly.

Examples and Case Studies

Considering these positive outcomes, more businesses intend to use AI in 2024 to bolster their marketing departments and advance their overarching business plans. Here are some of the most noteworthy uses of AI in marketing to help you make the most of social media marketing in 2024.

Examining data from social media
An abundance of brand and customer insights may be found in social media data, which AI systems can easily mine for important information. According to the State of Social Media Report, 95% of executives use social data to guide choices about competitor analysis, product creation, and lead generation. As a result, social media data analysis is strengthening cross-functional teams in addition to marketing teams.

According to the survey, 92% of business leaders believe that competitor monitoring would be crucial for improving brand positioning in 2024.

AI technologies use other AI algorithms and robust semantic search to derive competition insights from social listening data. For instance, Sprout uses named entity recognition (NER) to scan social data to find and examine rival brands and their content, giving you useful information to boost your brand's performance.

Using keywords and @mentions you choose, the capability delves into rival content engagements, post frequency, hashtag usage, and other critical performance areas. As a result, it can quickly sort through the thousands of social media conversations to provide you with information that is relevant to your company.

Influencer marketing is another important field. In order to assess potential influencers' appropriateness for brand relationships, marketers can use AI models to analyze their postings, interactions, and audience demographics. This convergence of social data analysis and AI capabilities to handle intelligence, reporting, and workflows for influencer marketing is further cemented by Sprout's recent acquisition of Tagger.

Producing content
According to the 2023 Index, one of the things that takes marketers the longest to complete is creating content. Time and mental space are not only wasted on creative ideation; there's also the pressure to make sure the information is fresh, relevant, interesting, and unique enough to keep viewers from scrolling on.

Fortunately, social media managers and teams can avoid the drawbacks of generic AI technologies by using specialized AI-enabled social management solutions for content creation and ideation.

For instance, Sprout's Suggestions by AI Assist function provides you with three outgoing copy options to help you quickly write compelling, brand-tailored articles. With the use of natural language processing (NLP), Sprout is able to comprehend the subtleties found in social chatter.

Based on this understanding, the platform recommends relevant content that generates quality leads and higher conversion rates.
Marketing teams may thus focus more of their time on creating successful campaigns while also maximizing the impact of their social media approach.

Campaign targeting and social media advertising

Two important applications of AI in marketing are social media advertising and campaign reporting. By examining audience preferences and engagement patterns, marketers are able to leverage AI to enhance social media advertising and make ads more visually appealing to viewers.

For instance, this Coca-Cola campaign creates an engaging advertisement movie by fusing generative AI with a compelling storytelling style.

Ad campaigns may now be continually optimized by machine learning (ML) algorithms, which automatically run A/B tests on various ad variations to determine which aspects work best for certain client categories. More tailored, targeted advertisements result from this. In order to improve campaign targeting and performance, AI-powered insights combined with predictive analytics automatically recommend pertinent goods and services based on previous user interactions.

With all of these benefits, marketers may increase the effectiveness of paid advertising and target audiences more precisely in a shorter amount of time than they would need to manually review and tweak the results.

In a similar vein, AI systems can produce dynamic advertisements that, in response to user activity and selection, dynamically update product details and prices. By doing this, you can increase your return on investment (ROI) and spare your marketing team the tiresome work of manually monitoring and modifying ad wording.

Take a look at Sprout's social ad reporting features to increase return on investment from the sponsored content you're planning.

Scheduling and posting on social media
Social media teams have to balance a number of tasks, such as promptly answering questions and concerns from users and making sure they don't forget to schedule material and publish by the deadline. For this reason, social media marketers aim to plan their posts and schedules far in advance so they can better prioritize campaigns and oversee team productivity.

AI marketing solutions save teams time and effort by precisely and smoothly automating these tasks. For instance, by figuring out when to publish on social media to get the most views and engagement from your audience, Sprout's AI capabilities automate social media scheduling and posting. In order to guarantee the best possible post interaction, machine learning algorithms examine engagement data over time and offer a variety of scheduling options, including recommendations for hashtags and ideal send times.

This gives advertisers the ability to accurately plan, arrange, and schedule social media messages using data on networks like Facebook, Instagram, and LinkedIn.

Developing conversational AI
One interesting application of AI in marketing is chatbots. Additionally, according to the 2023 Index, 54% of marketers intend to utilize them extensively for social customer service in 2024, in addition to other tools like FAQs and customer forums.

With chatbots, organizations can respond to consumer inquiries 24/7 by providing personalized, real-time interactions. Considering that 23% of consumers want businesses to answer within two hours and 16% expect brands to respond immediately, this goes a long way toward improving customer satisfaction and developing strong brand relationships.

As they process more data and compile insightful information about user behavior, chatbots powered by machine learning and neural networks get wiser. However, these virtual agents require monitoring, training, and adaptation to your tech stack. Sephora, a makeup brand, employs AI chatbot Kik to communicate with its consumers and to promote engagement through live influencer interactions.

Conversely, rules-based chatbots are easier to use. They allow brands to be available to their customers around-the-clock and are simple to set up in a matter of minutes.

You may increase efficiency tenfold by using a chatbot, such as Sprout's rules-based chatbot or an AI-enabled one, to answer product inquiries, make recommendations, and lead customers through the sales funnel even when your marketing team isn't accessible. Is there anything more ideal for customer service than that?

Measuring social media
These days, social performance statistics are an integral aspect of a brand's entire plan. In order to achieve their business objectives for 2024, an astounding 60% of marketers intend to track and assess the value of social engagements in terms of revenue effect.

Furthermore, according to 32% of marketers, they now share social metrics with their executive leadership once a week, reflecting the growing participation of leadership teams in a brand's social engine.

You may save hours of manual labor and performance analysis by using machine learning models like Sprout, which analyze quantitative and qualitative social indicators automatically and precisely in a matter of minutes. This is encouraging for marketers that wish to navigate the constantly shifting social media ecosystem and improve their return on investment.

Evaluation of sentiment
Sentiment analysis is being used by marketers to evaluate the tone and sentiment of postings, chats, and comments related to their brand in order to identify if the sentiment is neutral, positive, or negative. Given that, according to The State of Social Media Report, 44% of marketers utilize sentiment analysis to better analyze customer comments and respond to concerns, this is an essential AI capability.

Brands can identify early signs of bad sentiment and take proactive steps to address the situation before it gets out of hand by analyzing sentiment in social discourse.

For instance, you can track whether brand mentions are good or negative and identify anomalous spikes in Sprout. You may then keep an eye on your reputation to make sure your brand is doing well. Similar to this, incoming messages are tagged by sentiment analysis algorithms as good or negative so that your social customer service teams may prioritize them according to their importance.

In conclusion, social media marketing will undergo a transformation thanks to artificial intelligence starting in 2024. Marketers may improve consumer interaction, automate content creation, fine-tune targeting, track sentiment, and optimize influencer partnerships by utilizing AI-driven technology. Businesses who take advantage of these developments as AI develops will have a competitive advantage, strengthening relationships with their target market and improving social media marketing outcomes

Case Studies

AI-powered personalization is being used by a lot of companies these days to enhance customer experience and boost revenue. Here are a few noteworthy instances.

- Netflix offers its subscribers a streaming service that allows them to watch TV series, films, documentaries, and other content. The business uses machine learning algorithms to suggest movies and TV series to its customers based on their viewing tastes and history. Approximately 80% of the platform's streaming hours are covered by these personalized recommendations, which have significantly increased customer engagement and retention. Netflix has been able to expand and keep users for longer by customizing the user experience to each person's preferences.

- Sephora is a multinational corporation with a focus on marketing and selling cosmetics. The business is giving its clients a more engaging and customized purchasing experience by utilizing AI-powered personalization. In particular, the business analyzes consumers' face traits using machine learning algorithms to suggest makeup products that are appropriate for them. Because customers who use this recommendation tool are more likely to make a purchase than those who do not, Sephora has stated that the technology has enhanced customer happiness and confidence.

- Offering a wide range of goods and services to consumers, Amazon is the top worldwide e-commerce business. The company recommends products to its consumers based on their browsing and purchase history using AI-powered customisation. According to Amazon, the company's overall income has increased by up to 35% since the recommendation system was implemented.

Trend 2: Augmented Reality (AR) Experiences

Businesses' social media interactions with their customers are changing due to augmented reality (AR). By overlaying digital features on the actual environment, augmented reality (AR) creates immersive and interactive experiences that spark interaction, grab attention, and raise brand awareness.

Augmented reality, or AR, will still influence how we use social media in 2024.

With the use of this dynamic technology, users can have immersive and interactive experiences by superimposing digital objects onto the real world.

AR elements are being incorporated into social media platforms more and more, and in the upcoming year, this trend is predicted to pick up speed. On social media sites like Instagram and TikTok, augmented reality (AR) filters, effects, and lenses have already gained popularity. These tools let users add creative overlays, amusing masks, and animated elements to their pictures.

By 2024, augmented reality (AR) is predicted to have a far bigger impact, changing the way consumers engage with brands and information while creating new opportunities for marketing and innovation.

The line between real-world and virtual realities will become more hazy in 2024 as social media platforms develop their augmented reality capabilities, opening up new avenues for customer interaction, storytelling, and brand awareness.

Companies that are able to use this technology in innovative and creative ways will be at the forefront of innovation and will be recognized as digital pioneers.

How to Use AR in Your Social Media Marketing Plan for 2024

AR Lenses and Filters
Make customized AR filters and lenses that complement the tone and personality of your company.

With the help of these filters, social media users may include branded components in their images and videos, which raises user engagement and brand visibility.

Virtual Try-Ons: Offer augmented reality-enabled virtual try-ons if you sell apparel, cosmetics, or accessories.

Customers will feel more confident in their purchases if you let them try on your products before they buy them.

Improved Product Displays
Make interactive product demos with augmented reality.

AI, for instance, might be used by a furniture store to let clients place virtual furniture in real living rooms using the cameras on their smartphones to see how it fits and looks.

gamified encounters.
Make gamified or augmented reality games that highlight your items or brand. Playful and interactive user engagement strategies can boost engagement and brand recognition.

Your business may take use of the immersive and interactive qualities of this technology to create unique and captivating experiences for your audience, hence enhancing brand loyalty and increasing conversions, by implementing these AR methods into your 2024 digital marketing campaigns.

One Tree Planted: AR Done Correct.

Using the Tree Planter filter, One Tree Planted, an environmental nonprofit committed to reforestation, has cleverly incorporated augmented reality into its social media approach.

Using this Instagram filter, users may digitally plant trees by arranging them in a forest.

By making planting trees enjoyable and engaging, the Tree Planter filter inspires users to take practical action in addition to increasing awareness of the organization's fight against deforestation.

Users can apply AR filters to themselves or their surroundings to create fun and interesting experiences. This can be used to showcase features, market things, or just to amuse users.

Virtual try-ons: Customers can virtually try on things before making a purchase by utilizing augmented reality. This is especially helpful for products like makeup, eyewear, and apparel.

AR product demos: AR may be used to make interactive product demonstrations that let consumers see and engage with goods in a virtual setting. Through better understanding of products' functions, people can make more educated purchases.

AR experiences and games: Users can enjoy and share interactive games and experiences made possible by AR technology. This is a great method to keep users interested and coming back for more.

Advantages of Augmented Reality for Social Media Promotion:

Because AR offers users rich and interactive experiences they won't be able to refuse, it can assist to enhance engagement.

By giving consumers distinctive and memorable experiences that they will connect with your business, augmented reality (AR) can aid in raising brand awareness.

Sales growth: By enabling customers to digitally try on things and observe how they function before making a purchase, augmented reality can help boost sales.

Instances of Effective AR Campaigns in 2024.

The world is changing in many ways because of technology, and one of the most striking manifestations of this digital revolution is augmented reality, or AR. According to business analytics, over 60% of consumers think augmented reality (AR) improves shopping. Big corporations opted to offer consumers a new kind of marketing as soon as they realized this.

They developed augmented reality marketing strategies to draw in clients, setting the stage for a global trend of such initiatives. We'll examine 12 intriguing instances of augmented reality marketing in this piece. Let's investigate them!

IKEA AR Inventory

Being a well-known furniture brand, IKEA spends a lot of money on AR advertising.

IKEA introduced IKEA Place, an augmented reality software, in September 2017 that lets users virtually check out furniture. They can do this easily by looking around and placing their preferred furniture to see if it goes well with the space.

But now, all of this revolutionary change is accessible as an IKEA Kreativ feature that can be accessed straight through the IKEA app. With the app, users can quickly scan their space and use AR experiences powered by AI to arrange their preferred furniture.

In addition, you can practically remove any furniture that is currently in the space. This will provide you more room to arrange IKEA furniture and more creative freedom to design the area of your dreams.

Once the design is complete, you can easily inspect the products to see if they all fit and complement your ideas. If so, you may have them delivered straight to your door

IBM Shopping Application
IBM decided to improve its customers' in-store experience by developing an image recognition app. Customers can learn more about a product while shopping by taking a photo of the shelf. This type of augmented reality tool allows users to explore product information such as ingredients, protein count, prices, shelf dates, and so on.

According to retail specialists at the essay writing agency, the IBM shopping app elevates the consumer experience by allowing customers to make data-driven purchasing decisions in real time.

LCST: The Lacoste AR Retail Campaign
Engine Creative developed an innovative augmented reality solution for the LCST SS14 retail campaign. LCST, Lacoste's urban-savvy younger brother, is described as street style with a bite. As a brand, LCST is all about 'bringing the color', which necessitates a vibrant and innovative communications campaign to match.

The campaign allowed users to explore the colorful virtual world of LCST. Users simply scan trigger images available in-store to quickly test out the entire product line and interact with additional LCST content.

Thomas Cook: Try before you fly.
Thomas Cook, a UK-based travel agency, uses modern technology to improve their customers' experiences.

Consumers begin their journey in the cockpit of a Thomas Cook plane and can navigate to separate videos shot in economy and premium classes. The campaign's goal is to allow users to test out new planes and popular destinations before deciding where to travel. It's a simple yet effective example of how AR can be used as a marketing tool.

The Walking Dead Scary Shelter: Zombies Attack!
The Walking Dead team used a tram station in Vienna as the setting for their augmented reality trick. They promoted the fifth season of the

television show by superimposing a video layer on the station's glass wall.

The result was sensational: people could almost feel what it was like to face a zombie, eliciting strong emotional responses. It's a once-in-a-lifetime experience that leaves people with lasting memories of the Walking Dead.

Volvo Test Drive
Volvo designed an Augmented Reality experience for a YouTube masthead unit, allowing users to play the Augmented Reality Driving Game with their phones from within the banner.

This campaign brought the car to life on the YouTube homepage, generating significant media attention.

It received a 9.6% interaction rate and nearly 200 thousand clicks of engagement on the masthead unit, while Volvo increased its official website traffic by nearly 300%.

Although the brand is not as well-known as Mercedes-Benz or Ferrari, they outperformed their competitors with this campaign.

Converse: The Sampler iPhone App.
Another giant, on the other hand, has used augmented reality to provide users with an unforgettable shopping experience. The Sampler app allows users to virtually try on Converse classics and other collections.

After browsing the collections and selecting your favorite model, simply point your mobile camera towards your feet and scale the shoe to fit over your foot.

Absolut Vodka AR Application
Successful brands educate their customers in addition to selling them products. Absolut Vodka made a significant step forward in that regard by developing an augmented reality app that explains the brand's history.

Customers who purchased bottles with neck hangers could scan them and virtually visit the village of Ahus.
It is the birthplace of Absolut Vodka, and all ingredients are sourced from there. Aside from the visit, customers could observe the production process and receive free drink recipes.

The North Face
The North Face promoted its new line of winter coats by combining augmented reality and real-world effects. Sales representatives invited visitors to try on winter jackets, and the magic began.

The North Face used AR effects to take customers on a hiking tour through Yosemite National Park and Nepal. It's the ideal solution for adventurous consumers who want more than just quality when making a purchase decision.

Dutch Lady's Flying Farm
The Dutch Lady's Flying Farm app is an augmented reality mobile application created to support the milk brand's summer campaign in 2015. Their goal

was to encourage children to interact and engage with the brand.

By scanning the milk pack, children were transported to a virtual Dutch Lady farm with a variety of amusing features.

However, they had to collect 30 different packs to gain access to all options. The app was a huge success, generating over 40,000 downloads and increasing product sales by 19%.

American Apparel's Color-Changing App
American Apparel has a large selection of colorful products, but it can be difficult to choose the one that best suits your needs. That's why the company created this AR app, which allows for color-changing trials.

Store visitors can simply scan the product to see it in various colors and read reviews from other customers who have purchased the same item. It isn't a complicated AR project, but it works well and serves its purpose.

Strategies for Implementing Augmented Reality in Social Media Marketing

How many advertising messages do consumers receive every day? According to Carlos Arango, CEO of agency Sancho Bbdo, "Some studies suggest that a person can receive between 3,000 and 5,000 advertising messages from the moment they wake up."

In a world where consumers' attention spans are shrinking, creative directors and innovation leaders must find new ways to capture attention and make an impact. Augmented Reality (AR) is a tool that can help creative agencies and businesses overcome this obstacle.

AR enables the overlay of digital elements onto reality, resulting in more immersive and engaging experiences. This can help brands differentiate themselves from competitors and connect with customers more deeply. Watch the video below to learn more about this technology.

How to Lead an Effective Augmented Reality Implementation?

Virtual Reality (VR) has evolved from a futuristic technology to a powerful marketing tool, transforming the way brands interact with their customers.

When it comes to incorporating Augmented Reality (AR) into creative campaigns, it's critical to go beyond the basics and address advanced strategies to make an impact.

Think of augmented reality as a tool, not an end in itself.Augmented reality is a powerful tool for creating unique and memorable experiences. However, it's important to remember that augmented reality is only a tool. It is not a magical solution to all marketing issues.Before implementing AR in a campaign, agencies should think about how it can help achieve the campaign's goals. Will augmented reality help increase brand awareness? How do I generate leads? Drive sales?Once you've identified the campaign's objectives, you can start thinking about how AR can help you achieve them.

Strategic Immersion in the Product: AR is more than just overlaying virtual elements on physical reality; it is about how those elements improve the utility or user experience of a product or service. Agencies can lead this approach by considering how AR can be integrated into the product itself. This could include creating AR user manuals, interactive tutorials, or even AR features that help customers solve real-world problems.

Advanced Personalization: Personalization is a growing trend in marketing and advertising, and augmented reality provides exciting opportunities in this area. Creative directors can oversee the collection and analysis of user data in order to tailor AR experiences to specific preferences and needs. This not only boosts engagement, but also fosters a stronger connection with the audience.

AR is capable of multisensory interaction beyond vision. To create a more profound and memorable impact, agencies can investigate how to incorporate other senses, such as sound or touch, into AR experiences. Imagine a campaign in which users can interact with virtual objects or listen to immersive narratives. These multisensory experiences can have a lasting impact.

Integrating Augmented Reality into Omnichannel Campaigns Consistency is essential for a successful marketing strategy. You can ensure that AR experiences are seamlessly integrated across all customer touchpoints, including online, in-store, and live events. This ensures that the brand sends a consistent and powerful message.

Advanced Data Analysis: Data collection is critical in AR implementation. Creative directors can lead the use of advanced data analytics to better understand how users interact with augmented reality experiences. This not only allows for accurate performance evaluation, but it also provides useful insights for future improvements and strategy adjustments.

Exploration of New Contexts and Virtual Spaces: Augmented reality is not limited to the physical world; it can also be applied to the virtual world. Creative directors can take the lead in exploring new contexts, such as the metaverse and virtual reality, and determining how AR can fit into these emerging environments. Early adaptation to new platforms can provide exciting opportunities to reach audiences in novel ways.

Strategic Partnerships: No one has all of the answers, and augmented reality is a constantly evolving field. Creative directors can take the lead in identifying strategic partnerships with technology companies or creators of augmented reality content. These collaborations can provide additional resources, technical expertise, and access to cutting-edge technology, accelerating the use of augmented reality in campaigns.

Case Study and Examples

Fender's AR Activation Campaign.
The case study of Fender and R/GA in collaboration with AR creator Florian Sabatier demonstrates how this technology can elevate interaction and user experience.

Jeremy Cox, Group Creative Director at R/GA, believes that augmented reality provides an unparalleled blank canvas for brands. It enables the convergence of visual, auditory, and motion elements in the real world, immersing users in a unique experience.

R/GA and Fender collaborated to create an exciting augmented reality effect that overlayed a virtual guitar into the user's physical world, allowing them to play it with movements. This innovative AR experience elevated Fender's brand narrative to a whole new level.

Jeremy Cox provides essential tips for brands looking to use augmented reality. First and foremost, ensure that AR is appropriate for the campaign's objectives and target audience. It should not be used solely for the sake of being trendy, but because it has the potential to create a unique and effective experience.

Furthermore, the user experience should be seamless and simple in order to engage and guide people through the process. Finally, working with an innovative AR development partner is essential for overcoming technical limitations and creating incredible experiences.

Trend 3: Video Content Dominance

In the digital age, videotape content has become an essential part of marketing since it engages observers and boosts engagement further than any other media. videos are really a great tool for marketing since they offer an engaging way to show products, communicate ideas, and engage observers with emotionally charged stories.

Examining the function of videotape in content marketing makes it clear that this isn't just a fleeting trend, but rather a abecedarian shift in how associations communicate with their target request. Thanks to the growth of digital platforms, videotape content is now more accessible and switching, and businesses of all kinds are taking advantage of this to reach a wider followership.

Unlike other forms of information, videotape provides an immersive experience that strengthens the connection between the bystander and the business, leaving a more continuing print. videotape content is a significant player in the competitive digital assiduity, as seen by its capacity to transfigure marketing strategies. A Statista bean indicates that the profit from videotape advertising reached $176.6 billion in 2023 and is predicted to grow at a rate of 6.49 each time until 2028. The average existent in 2023 watched 17 hours of digital videos every week, and 92.3 percent of internet druggies participated in this geste. videotape marketing has been around for a long time and will keep evolving through 2024.

As requests expand and technology evolves, new trends in social media videotape marketing are always being seen. This includes TikTok's request dominance and the growing fashionability of short-form flicks on platforms like Facebook and Instagram.

Companies may always come up with innovative and fresh approaches to engage implicit guests and boost profit. You can lose out on advancements in videotape advertising if you are not informed. videotape content is king as we enter the always-evolving field of digital marketing.

The significance of noteworthy and engaging videos in 2024 can not be exaggerated. Businesses must use slice-edge videotape marketing strategies and trends that appeal to their target demographic. In the moment's fast-paced digital world, videotape content is getting incredibly popular on social networking sites. Because videotape is dynamic and amusing, it has become the format of choice for both individualities and associations to interact with their cult.

This book will look at the rearmost trends and stylish practices girding the spread of videotape content on social media. The Impact of videos on Social Media Videos convey dispatches, elicit important feelings, and tell tales in a manner that other forms of media just can not match. With social media platforms continuing to punctuate videotape content, businesses, and influencers can now use it as an important tool to interact with their target followership.

First Fashion Live streaming Several social media platforms have seen an increase in the fashionability of live broadcasting. druggies can partake guests in real- time, engage directly with their followership, and establish meaningful connections thanks to it. Whether it's a product preface, a Q&A session, or a before- the- scenes peep, live broadcasting encourages exclusivity and enables instant engagement.

Short videos are the Alternate TrendThe rise of platforms like TikTok and Instagram Reels has unnaturally altered how we consume videos. Short-form videos, which generally run between 15 and 60 seconds, are getting increasingly popular due to their bite- sized format and quick entertainment value. products and generators are using these platforms to showcase their gift, reach a youngish followership, and promote their products.

Using videos to Tell Stories is the Third TrendVideos offer an absorbing system to tell stories, which has long been an important marketing strategy. By adding a story to their videotape content, brands may be suitable to forge a near emotional connection with their observers. This tactic promotes brand fidelity, followership participation, and long- lasting goods.

The Growth of Viral Content on Social Media spots It's insolvable for a lot of businesses, marketers, and content directors to go viral on socialmedia.Increased income, guests, and followers could be affected from increased commerce, visibility, and reach.

However, getting viral is a gruelling accomplishment. With so important material being created and participated every day, it can be gruelling to stand out and snare people's attention. In 2024, the viral geography will continue to shift and develop. New platforms will crop , algorithms will shift, and trends will come andgo.To succeed in this terrain, marketers and content generators must stay up to date on the newest strategies, tactics, and stylish practices for viral content. They must also be willing to take chances, try new effects, and learn from both their lapses and successes. Understanding the contagious terrain To go viral in 2024, one needs to have a solid understanding of the digital geography and the factors that contribute to virality. Then there are many pivotal points to keep in mind about the conduct of algorithms. Algorithms largely mandate the content that druggies view on social media platforms like Facebook, Instagram, TikTok, YouTube, Twitter, andLinkedIn.

Understanding these algorithms and the factors they take into account will help you produce content that has a lesser possibility of getting viral. For illustration, the TikTok algorithm favors videos with high completion rates, trendy noises, and hashtags. opting Your Target Market Knowing who your target followership is will help you produce material that will intrigue them. This means paying attention to their age, gender, interests, and geste.

By producing content specifically for your target followership, you may increase the liability that they will engage with and partake it. assaying Current Trends and Market Keeping up with new requests and trends will help you produce content that has a better possibility of getting viral. This means keeping an eye on trending noises, applicable hashtags, and popular content orders. It's imperative, however, to make sure your target request and brand are compatible with the trends and commerce you are keeping an eye on.

The Impact of Social Media Platforms

Your content's potential to go viral might be affected by the audiences and algorithms of various social media platforms.

For instance, LinkedIn is more suited for professionals, whereas TikTok is more popular with younger audiences.

You can produce content that is optimized for each platform by having a thorough understanding of the distinct characteristics and target audiences of each one.

Formats and Types of Content

Your content's format and type can have an effect on how viral it becomes.

For instance, video material frequently has a higher level of engagement and shareability than text postings or still photos.

Because they can draw viewers in and give context for your material, captions and descriptions can also have an impact on how viral your content becomes.

Participation and Community

Creating a community around your brand and interacting with your audience might help make your content more viral.

Engaging with your fans, participating in pertinent communities, and working together with other influencers and content producers are all examples of this.

Content Creators' Influence

Influencers and content producers can also have a big impact on how viral your material becomes.

You can expand the reach of your material by collaborating with social media managers, influencers, and other content providers to take advantage of their pre-existing followers.

In general, it will be crucial to comprehend the subtleties of the digital environment and produce content that is tailored to your target audience and the social media channels you are utilizing in 2024 if you want it to become viral.

You may raise the chance that your material will go viral by keeping up with the latest trends and niches, interacting with your audience, and utilizing the power of influencers and content creators.

Creating Content That Goes Viral

Although producing viral content is not a precise science, there are some factors that can make a post more likely to become viral.

The most crucial elements to take into account when creating viral content are examined in the next subsections.

Crafting a Powerful Hook

It is crucial to begin with an attention-grabbing and captivating hook in order to capture the viewer's attention.

A humorous meme, a catchy phrase, or an eye-catching image can all serve as hooks.

Making sure the hook is pertinent to the material and will persuade the viewer to continue watching is crucial.

Creating Superior Content

When it comes to producing material that goes viral, quality matters more than quantity.

Producing one excellent piece of content is preferable to 10 subpar ones.

Content that has value has a higher chance of being shared and interacted with, which can aid in its viral growth.

Making Use of Sounds and Music

Content can be given a new depth and made more engaging by using music and noises.

Employing popular music and sounds can help content remain current and appeal to a larger audience.

Including Useful Hashtags and Captions

Hashtags and captions are crucial for increasing the discoverability of information.

While well-written subtitles can captivate viewers and entice them to share the material, relevant hashtags can help content reach a larger audience.

When to Post

The optimal timing of posts is crucial for optimizing interaction and raising the likelihood of material becoming viral.

It's critical to investigate the optimal posting timings on various social media platforms as they all have distinct peak hours.

Taking Part in Community Activities

Participating in the community is crucial for gaining followers and raising the likelihood that a piece of content will become viral.

A devoted following can be developed and engagement levels raised by interacting with other artists, sharing their material, and responding to comments left by them.

Making the Most of User Interactions

Likes, comments, and shares from users are crucial indicators that a content is connecting with readers.

Promoting viewer interaction with material can boost interest and raise the likelihood that it will become viral.

Adjusting to Specific Platforms

When it comes to content, many social media sites have varying criteria and preferences.

Content that is tailored to the platform will engage users more and have a greater possibility of becoming viral.

Search and Discovery Optimization

Increasing visibility and the likelihood that a piece of content will become viral needs optimizing it for search and discovery using SEO.

Search engine and social media platform exposure and ranking can be improved by using relevant keywords, improving descriptions, and making sure information is easily discoverable.

Optimizing Outreach and Involvement

In 2024, maximizing reach and interaction on social media platforms will be crucial for a content to become viral.

This can be accomplished in a number of ways, including by being aware of platform algorithms, developing a large following, promoting shares and vitality, utilizing analytics to guide strategy, working with other creators, taking part in challenges and trends, replying to engagement and comments, and improving content in response to feedback.

Knowing How Platform Algorithms Work

Social media networks display content to users based on algorithms. Comprehending these algorithms is essential for optimizing outreach and interaction.

For instance, content with a high view time, trending sounds, and engagement is given priority by the TikTok algorithm.

Conversely, content that garners a lot of likes, comments, and shares is given priority by the Instagram algorithm.

material producers can enhance their chances of going viral by customizing their material by knowing these algorithms.

Establishing a Robust Following

To maximize reach and engagement, you need a sizable following.

High-quality content that connects with and motivates their target audience to follow should be the creators' main priority.

They should also interact with their fans by leaving comments and sending direct messages, as well as by following and interacting with other creators in their industry.

Promoting Virality and Shares

Viraility and shares are essential for content creators. The goal for content creators should be to provide engaging and shareable material.

Using hashtags, producing timely and relevant material, and working with other creators to create viral content are some ways to accomplish this.

Using Analytics to Guide Strategy

Analytics can offer insightful information about the effectiveness of content and audience participation.

In order to monitor the number of followers, engagement rates, and video performance, creators need to use analytics.

Future strategy and content can be informed by this information.

Working Together with Other Artists

Partnering with other artists can help expand your audience and boost interaction.

In order to collaborate with other creators in their specialty, creators should seek out opportunities such as joint content creation or participation in challenges.

Taking Part in Trends and Challenges

Reach and engagement can be greatly increased by taking part in challenges and trends.

It's important for creators to be abreast of current trends and take part in challenges that are pertinent to their industry.

Answering Questions and Taking Input

Building a solid following requires interaction and response to comments.

To develop a devoted fan base, creators should make the time to answer questions and interact with their followers.

Content Adjustment Based on Reactions

In order to improve content and boost engagement, feedback is crucial.

In order to improve the resonance of their material with their audience, creators ought to pay attention to the input provided by their followers.

In 2024, content creators can boost their chances of going viral by producing captivating material and cultivating a sizable fan base.

Maintaining Internet Trends

Increasing sales, expanding a company account, and raising brand exposure are all made possible by becoming viral.

To guarantee long-term growth and success, it is equally crucial to maintain viral success. The following are some tactics to maintain viral success:

Adapting to the Platform and Viewers

Since social media sites like TikTok are always changing, it's critical to keep up with the newest functionalities and fashions.

Knowing your target audience and producing insightful material that appeals to them are also essential.

material creators can continue to produce interesting and viral material by staying up to date with the platform and their audience.

Sustaining Uniformity and Excellence

Maintaining viral success requires consistency and high quality.

It is recommended that creators keep a content calendar and adhere to a consistent publication schedule.

Prioritizing quality above quantity and producing meaningful content that is consistent with the brand and message are also crucial.

Maintaining Your Message and Brand Integrity

Remaining loyal to the brand and message is another requirement for maintaining viral success.

Content producers need to make sure that their work reflects the message and values of the brand.

Creators can develop a devoted following and raise brand exposure by doing this.

Transforming Virtuality into Commercial Possibilities

A viral video can result in a number of commercial opportunities, such as sales, sponsorships, and brand partnerships.

Creators ought to take use of their virality in order to expand their company accounts and turn it into commercial prospects.

Developing a Long-Term Content Strategy

For a content strategy to remain viral, it must be long-term.

In order to make sure that their content calendar is consistent with the brand and message, creators should plan it out in advance.

By doing this, content producers can keep producing interesting, shareable, and audience-relevant content.

Respecting Community Guidelines

Following community rules is essential to maintaining viral success.

The guidelines and policies of the platform should be familiar to creators, and they should make sure that their work complies with them.

Creators can prevent having their accounts suspended or having their content erased by doing this.

Preventing Burnout and Maintaining Inspiration

Lastly, artists need to maintain their inspiration and prevent burnout. Being popular can be overwhelming, so artists should prioritize self-care and take pauses as needed.

By doing this, content producers can keep producing interesting, shareable, and audience-relevant content.

Handling the Difficulties of Going Viral

It's not as simple as it seems to create viral content. It requires a great deal of imagination, time, and work.

But even with the greatest material, trying to go viral still presents difficulties for content producers. We'll talk about some of the difficulties associated with becoming viral in this part, along with solutions.

Handling Rivalry

When it comes to going viral, competition is one of the main obstacles. It might be challenging to stand out when there are so many individuals producing material.

Content producers must figure out how to set themselves apart from rivals in order to survive the competition.

This can be achieved by focusing on a particular audience, creating original content, or developing a strong brand identity.

Creating aesthetically pleasing and captivating material is one method to set oneself apart from rivals.

This can be accomplished by utilizing top-notch photos and videos in addition to adding interactive features like surveys and quizzes.

Recognizing the Dangers of Virality

Going viral has hazards even if it can sometimes be advantageous.

One of the largest dangers is that the audience won't find the content appealing, which could result in unfavorable comments and harm to the brand's reputation.

Going viral can sometimes draw unwelcome attention and criticism from rival websites or online trolls.

Content producers must be conscious of the possible repercussions of their work going viral and take action to reduce them in order to reduce these risks.

This can be achieved by keeping a close eye on the material and promptly and expertly handling any unfavorable comments.Content producers should also have a crisis management strategy ready in case their work is met with backlash.

In conclusion, if you want to start a viral trend in 2024, you should concentrate on producing original, captivating content. The trend's reach can also be expanded by working with other influencers, interacting with followers, and using social media channels to promote it. When creating content, it's critical to maintain consistency and try out various forms to find what works best for your audience.

Using Videotape Content to Its Fullest Implicit for Marketing Success

Why Make Pretensions for Social Media?

1. Guidance and Concentration Your social media sweats can be directed in a certain direction by using pretensions as a roadmap. They give your strategy a distinct emphasis, keeping it from getting disorganized or inconsistent.

2. Measurable Achievement Measurable objects let you cover your progress and fete accomplishments. Success can be quantified by criteria like conversion rates, follower growth, and engagement rates.

3. Engagement of the followership Setting pretensions will help you produce material that appeals to your intended followership. To have a significant online presence, you must comprehend the tastes and habits of your followership.

The SMART Method for Establishing pretensions

In order to make sure your social media objects are successful, you must cleave to the SMART frame. Particularly:

1. Establish precise, well-defined pretensions for your social media approach. For case In the first quarter, raise Instagram engagement by 30.

2. Quantifiable Set up measures that will let you gauge your success. Example: By the end of the time, get 1,000 new Instagram followers.

3. Realistic: Make sure your pretensions are ambitious but realizable. As an illustration, start a tri weekly blog post series without immolating happy quality.

4. material Make sure your objects line up with your overarching commercial pretensions. As an illustration, use social media to increase website business and deals.

5. Temporal Boundaries Decide on a deadline for finishing each task. For case Start a podcast by the end of the alternate quarter.

Creating Your 2024 Social Media Objective

1. Boost Recognition of Your Brand Make use of social media channels to raise mindfulness of your brand. Use ways like focused hashtags, eye-catching images, and harmonious branding.

2. Encourage followership participation. Use interactive content to help you and your followership make deeper connections. suppose about using checks, tests, and Q&A sessions to boost involvement.

3. Increased transformations produce a plan to turn followers on social media into guests. Make use of smooth stoner gests, exclusive promos, and eye-catching calls to action.

4. Diversification of Content transfigures current material into new forms to reach a larger followership. Try using live sessions, infographics, and vids to keep your information intriguing.

The Significance of thickness in Social Media

1. **Establishes Credibility and Trust**: Regular blogging builds followership trust by demonstrating your responsibility and commitment. Harmonious updates are essential for an authentic and secure web presence.

2. **Increases Brand mindfulness:** Numerous platforms have algorithms that award regular content directors. Harmonious publishing improves brand visibility by adding the liability that your material will show up in the feeds of your followership.

3. **Encouraging Involvement from the followership:** Maintaining thickness helps your followership flash back your brand. Active followers are more likely to engage with your material, spread the word about it, and end up as devoted patrons.

Practical Advice for Upholding Social Media Regularity

1. **Establish a Content timetable**: Produce a yearly or daily content timetable to help you plan your content ahead of time. This guarantees that your social media trials will be regular and well-planned.

2. **Maintain an advertisement timetable**: Establish the stylish times to post on every platform. Maintaining a regular advertisement schedule makes it easier for compendiums to anticipate and look forward to your content.

3. **Expand the Variety of Your Content**: Maintain a different content blend to accommodate a range of tastes. To keep people interested, try different effects like filmland, vids, checks, and behind-the- scenes aesthetics .

4. **Interact with the followership**: Reply as soon as possible to mentions, dispatches, and commentary. Engage in discussion laboriously to make a feeling of community around your brand.

5. **Track Analytics and Make adaptations**: Dissect your data frequently to find out what resonates most

with your followership. To optimize your content strategy, make necessary adaptations depending on performance statistics. It's time to put your newfound understanding of the significance of thickness and thing- setting on social media into practice. Consider your company's pretensions for a moment, also produce SMART social media pretensions that support your 2024 vision.

Innovative styles and Stylish Practices

1. Fete Your Target request: Who might be your target clientele? Who needs or wants your products, and why? Still, start by conducting followership exploration, If you intend to use social media for a super-eminent generation.

Try to learn further about them than just their demographic's abecedarian characteristics. Rather than viewing your guests as followership demographics, begin to see them as factual people with requirements, interests, and problems.

You can construct a buyer persona and organize your client data also to how you would a character to gain a better understanding of who your consumers are.

You must be apprehensive of the following details about your guests in order to produce a buyer persona pursuits and interests Values Purchase patterns Difficulties and pain points pretensions requirements and solicitations favorite social media platforms kinds of material they like Their primary shopping and content consumption bias

2. Review Your Online Image on Social Media

You have to start with the man in the mirror if you want to get better. Although that seems corny, it's true.

To develop a successful social media plan, you must assess your performance and identify your advantages and disadvantages. Take on the mindset of an authentic social media marketer!

You will then be aware of what needs to change and what you should keep doing.

The steps to doing a social media audit are as follows:

Verify the accuracy and completeness of the information you post on your social media profiles.

Look for and report any fake accounts that appear to be using your brand.

Keep an eye on your reach, likes, comments, shares, and see which of your posts are doing the best.

Examine your analytics to determine the demographics of your social media followers.

Examine your activity data to identify areas for improvement.

Determine which social media networks you should stick with and which ones you should give up on by comparing the performance of each one.

Analyze the ROI and effectiveness of your social media advertising.

3. Employ SocialBee or other Social Media Management Tools

It can take a lot of time to manage several social media accounts at once since you have to actively produce and publish material on each channel.

Therefore, using scheduling tools to automate content production and distribution duties can save you hours of labor every week, regardless of whether you are a social media firm handling hundreds of clients or a small business owner that lacks the time to manage their social media presence.

With SocialBee, users can manage all of their social media accounts from one location by creating, scheduling, and posting material to each one individually.

You may alter the word count, add hashtags, emoticons, and change the picture sizes of your images in your social media posts from a single content editor to make them suitable for every platform.

Additionally, by gaining access to your analytics with SocialBee, you can keep an eye on how well you're performing on social media. Additionally, you can invite your team members to SocialBee and set up distinct workspaces for each of your businesses so that you can collaborate and produce interesting content on the same platform.

Other SocialBee capabilities that can assist you in producing better content faster are as follows:

Sort your social media posts according to subjects.

Create a unique posting schedule for every social media platform you use.

Establish evergreen posting schedules to keep your social media postings flowing consistently.

Get suggestions for well chosen material in the SocialBee post categories.

Use the Canva Integration to create visual content directly from SocialBee's content editor.

a visual calendar-style overview of your social media content strategy.

1. Know Your Audience: Recognize the tastes, passions, and demographics of your target market. Make sure your video material speaks to them in a meaningful way.

2. Keep It Brief and Interesting: Social media users' attention spans are short. Make sure that your films are brief, interesting, and direct in order to grab the attention of your viewers in the first few seconds.

3. Make Mobile Friendly: The majority of people who utilize social media do so via mobile devices. Make sure your movies include crisp images, readable text, and the right structure for mobile devices.

4. Add captions: To make your movies more accessible and to ensure that a wider audience sees your message, you must include subtitles. Additionally, it facilitates audience interaction with your content in settings when audio may not be possible.

5. Make Use of Eye-Catching Thumbnails: Your video's thumbnail serves as its entry point. Make visually beautiful and pertinent thumbnails to draw viewers in and encourage them to click through to your content.

6. Experiment with Different Formats: Don't be scared to experiment with various video formats, including user-generated material, interviews, tutorials, and behind-the-scenes videos. You can find what appeals to your audience the most by experimenting and maintaining the freshness of your material.

7. Call-to-Action: Ensure that your films conclude with a clear call to action. Point viewers in the direction of the next action, whether that is to visit your website, sign up for your channel, or leave a remark.

In conclusion, the emergence of video content on social media is changing the way we interact with brands and how we consume information. Businesses and individuals may use video to connect, inspire, and expand their online presence by adhering to current trends and putting best practices into effect. Take part in the revolution of visual storytelling and establish yourself in the fascinating realm of social media video production.

Recall that there are countless options when it comes to video. Now take out your camera, let your imagination go wild, and begin producing captivating films that will enthrall viewers on social media.

Trend 4: Influencer Collaboration Evolution

Since it first emerged more than ten years ago, influencer marketing has developed into a powerful force in the social media space. But will it still be applicable in 2024?

Influencer marketing: what is it?

Influencer marketing is a calculated strategy for promoting goods, services, or brands through partnerships with people who are well-known, knowledgeable, or have a sizable fan base in a specific market or sector. These people—known as influencers—endorse or suggest things to their devoted and engaged audience through blogs, social media platforms, and other online channels.
Influencer marketing leverages users' social media followings.

These 'influencers' have the power to affect their followers' buying decisions due to their prominence and authority on a particular platform.
Because they are dependable sources and trendsetters, influencers are becoming more and more important in today's marketing campaigns.

Influencer marketing is the practice of companies partnering with these well-known figures to advertise their goods or services. Influencer marketing is more than just finding an audience member and buying them to promote you; it's about relationships and genuineness.

Crucial elements of this approach include a strong collaborative relationship between the influencer and the brand they support, as well as strong and trustworthy ties between the influencer and their followers.

In order to ensure that the recommendations they give to their followers are genuine, influencers prefer to collaborate with brands they can rely on. The products or services that are recommended must not only be pertinent, but also genuine from the influencer. Influencer marketing campaigns need to add value to the followers' and target audience's online experiences in order to be successful.

A single product recommendation or reference has the potential to spark a comprehensive marketing campaign with multiple postings.

Important components that characterize influencer marketing:

- Influencers and their audience frequently have a relationship based on honesty and trust, which gives credibility to any recommendation.

- Influencers are often chosen on the basis of how well-suited they are to the target market of the brand.

- The number of followers an influencer has is not the only factor that determines their reach; audience engagement also plays a significant role.

- The effectiveness of influencer marketing campaigns depends heavily on the influencers' ability to interact with their audience and generate deep interactions centered around the brand's message.

- Targeting niche markets where the influencer has established authority is one of influencer marketing's benefits; this could result in higher conversion rates than broad-spectrum advertising.

The Transformation of Social Media Influencer Marketing

Businesses want to access a more genuine and relatable type of advertising by utilizing influencers' reach and credibility, which allows them to connect with potential customers in a manner that traditional advertising frequently cannot. Influencer marketing is a vital part of many contemporary marketing strategies since it can increase brand recognition, legitimacy, and customer involvement.

These influencer trends for 2024 are important to look at because influencer marketing is becoming more and more popular and costing more money. You'll then be able to decide where to concentrate your efforts and advertising budget to get the most returns.

1. Utilizing Various Social Media Channels and Cross-Platform Content Production

These days, a lot of content producers use multiple social media networks. It's amazing because they have a large following of incredibly loyal followers who follow them everywhere they upload.

Therefore, large audiences follow and comment on the work of successful creators across several media. They are specialists in their profession, and their admirers follow them all over the internet; they are not only renowned on one platform, like YouTube or Instagram. They select the platform that best suits their needs and goals. In a manner, everything is related even though they utilize various platforms for different purposes.

2. **In-person purchasing**
The practice of live shopping, in which goods are sold via social media live videos, has gained a lot of traction recently and is expected to continue expanding through 2024. Social media influencers and other well-known figures will continue to flaunt their lives and market products to their fans through interactive and live video content.

Live video sales are starting to gain popularity over other social media channels for product purchases. Large corporations are participating in it, including Amazon, Facebook, Instagram, and TikTok. Instagram, for instance, created "Live Shopping" so that you may make purchases directly from an Instagram Live broadcast. They claim it's awesome since shopping feels like you're actually there. Many well-known figures on the internet have been involved in live shopping and brand collaborations.

Therefore, it's likely that you'll witness a lot more of these collaborations in the upcoming year.

3. Extended Collaborations

In order to develop more enduring relationships and trust with their audience, brands may move away from one-time initiatives and toward long-term partnerships with influencers. Content that is cohesive and consistent with the brand's image is frequently the outcome of long-term relationships. This keeps the brand message consistent across various channels and initiatives. Influencers can give the company insightful feedback over time as a result of their interactions and experience with the audience. Companies can utilize this input to improve their target demographic targeting and marketing methods.

4. Shorter Videos Are More Common

We can't overlook the significance of short videos on social media nowadays, even though we've discussed them previously. Once the leader in short video content, TikTok has been challenged by rival apps like Instagram, Snapchat, and YouTube, who have entered the market with features like YouTube Shorts, Instagram Reels, and Snapchat Spotlight. As an alternative to TikTok, there's also an app called Triller that's really popular, especially in regions like India.

Presently, a lot of influencers are collaborating with marketers to create brief videos for all these platforms in order to convey their message in brief, visually appealing segments. To grab people's attention, material must be presented in digestible chunks.

5. **A focus on genuine influence**
In the field of influencer marketing, a prominent trend is the emphasis on authentic influence. This trend emphasizes how crucial transparency, sincerity, and authenticity are to influencer-brand collaborations. Genuine influencers don't only promote goods or services; they also share their own experiences and thoughts. They establish a deeper connection with their audience by sharing personal tales that they can relate to.

Genuine influencers also favor collaborating with companies that share their interests and values. Their audience respects them because they are picky about the connections they form and only endorse goods or causes that truly resonate with them. This movement is a reaction to how influencer marketing is changing and how customers are growing pickier and looking for more genuine relationships with the accounts they follow online.

6. Chief Influence Officers (CIOs) are introduced

One new influencer marketing trend that represents the growing significance of influencer cooperation inside companies is the appointment of Chief Influence Officers (CIOs). CIOs are strategic leaders that create and carry out influencer marketing plans that complement the goals of the brand. Their comprehension of the influencer market is extensive, encompassing the identification of suitable influencers, partnership negotiations, and campaign efficacy measurement. In order to smoothly include influencer marketing into the broader marketing plan, CIOs collaborate closely with other marketing divisions. They make sure influencer campaigns line up with larger marketing campaigns and brand messaging.

Organizations may fully realize the benefits of influencer partnerships, establish more genuine connections with their audience, and propel corporate growth in a world increasingly reliant on digital and social media by allocating senior positions to influencer marketing.

7. An increase in content created by employees

A prominent development in modern marketing and communication tactics is the advent of employee-generated content, wherein businesses encourage and utilize their staff members to produce and disseminate brand-related content. Consumers tend to view information created by employees as more authentic and reliable. Employee experiences, opinions, and insights about the business, its goods, or its culture are shared, and this adds an authentic element that is sometimes difficult to accomplish through conventional marketing.

Conversely, content created by employees offers a variety of perspectives from around the company. This diversity can show the company's dedication to inclusivity and diversity while also enabling it to engage with a wider audience. By giving the brand a face and personality, this kind of material humanizes the brand and makes it seem more approachable and relatable. In the digital age, employee-generated content can be a powerful tool for marketing, communication, and brand-building when done carefully and in line with the brand's values and goals.

Innovative Techniques for Working with Influencers

Identifying the Right Influencer for Your Brand

Selecting the ideal influencers for your brand is essential when it comes to influencer marketing. However, how do you approach it? Let's look at some essential actions you may do to make sure you locate the ideal fit.

Identifying your brand's values and target market

Establishing your target market and brand values is essential before launching an influencer marketing campaign. Finding influencers that share your values and connect with your audience can be made easier if you know who your ideal clients are and what your brand stands for.

For instance, if your sustainable fashion firm caters to millennials who are concerned about the environment, you should work with influencers who have similar goals and ideals. Your partnerships will be most effective and reach the intended audience in this way.

completing in-depth research to identify pertinent influences

It's time to do in-depth research to identify key influencers after you have determined your target market and brand values. This stage is searching industry-specific websites and social media platforms for influencers that are active in your sector and have a sizable following.

Investigate several channels and seek out influencers who regularly create excellent material that connects with their audience. To make sure they can properly convey your brand message, keep a careful eye on their interaction rates and the content's relevancy.

Take into account the kind of information they produce as well. Do they prioritize lifestyle, beauty, or fashion? Knowing their niche will enable you to assess whether their audience would be interested in your goods or services and whether their content is consistent with your brand.

Assessing influencers' veracity and sincerity

It's critical to consider an influencer's authenticity and reputation before partnering with them. Seek out influencers who regularly create excellent content and who truly connect with their audience.

Investigating their prior joint ventures is one method of evaluating their credibility. Have they collaborated with companies that share your beliefs? Do their joint ventures seem natural or forced? These are crucial inquiries to take into account while assessing the reliability of an influencer.

It's also important to look at the demographics of their followers. Make sure that the people that follow them are real, active, and part of your target market. It's important to consider the caliber of your followers and their level of interest in your business in addition to sheer quantity of followers.

You may find the ideal fit for your brand by carefully investigating and assessing influencers using these procedures. Recall that influencer marketing is all about reaching the proper audience and establishing real connections, so make your selections carefully!

Creating Fruitful Partnerships with Influencers
formulating a precise influencer marketing plan
Formulating a well-defined influencer marketing plan is vital prior to initiating any kind of cooperation. Describe your goals, specify your campaign's key performance indicators (KPIs), and set a budget. Choose the measures, such as reach, engagement, or conversions, that will be used to

gauge the effectiveness of your partnerships. You can make sure that your influencer relationships are successful in producing the results you want by establishing clear objectives and rules.

Forming Alliances That Will Benefit Both Parties

Establishing mutually beneficial partnerships is a prerequisite for building effective collaborations with influencers. Influencers should be included in the creative process and treated as important brand ambassadors. Let them use their imaginations, but make sure the stuff they produce reflects your brand. You may establish relationships that will benefit your brand and the influencers in the long run by building trust and encouraging open communication.

settling on conditions and payment with influencers
The conditions and payment should be discussed and negotiated when working with influencers. For every partnership, specify the deliverables, timetable, and extent of work in detail. Take into account the influencer's impact to your brand and provide just remuneration. Whether it's exclusive access, product samples, or cash payment, make

sure the conditions are favorable to both parties and meet the influencers' expectations.

Utilizing Various Influencer Types

Recognizing the various influencer categories

Knowing the many categories influencers fit into is crucial when working with them. Macro-influencers are good for spreading brand awareness because they usually have a sizable fan base and reach a broad audience. Conversely, micro-influencers provide a more focused approach because of their smaller but very active community. Selecting the kind of influencer that best fits your marketing objectives may be achieved by being aware of the advantages and disadvantages of each category.

Selecting the ideal influencer category for your campaign

Make sure the influencers you choose for your campaign are in line with your objectives and target demographic. Take into account their industry relevancy, specialization knowledge, and content style.

For instance, a fashion brand can gain from working with stylists or bloggers who can present their items in an approachable and aesthetically pleasing manner. You may increase the effectiveness of your influencer marketing initiatives by carefully selecting influencers that connect with your target audience and brand.

Working together with Nano and Micro Influencers

If you're unfamiliar with the idea of influencer marketing, you may think that more is always better. That isn't the case, though. Celebrity endorsements have decreased recently, and working with nano and micro influencers has taken their place. For many businesses, this shift has increased engagement and increased return on investment.

What benefits do nano and micro influencers offer? Is a huge influencer still valuable? Let's examine each one in turn.

Nano-influencers: Typically, they have between 1,000 and 5,000 followers. They have a growing following and are frequently new. These influencers are effective if your company is local or if your product is meant for a very particular market.

Your brand will be seen by the appropriate individuals if the nano influencer caters to the same demographic as your goods. Although their posts aren't as "perfect" or heavily edited as those of other influencers, these people are credible.

Moreover, these influencers have reduced cost-per-post expenses, which is beneficial if your campaign has a limited budget. As a matter of fact, you could merely ship your item and forego receiving payment. This typically occurs with influencers on Tik Tok who are just starting off with their profile.
Working with nano influencers has drawbacks because of their limited audience. Furthermore, they might not have the same time or resources as other types of influencers to produce a professional piece because this is typically not their primary role.

Micro influencers: Individuals with 5,000–50,000 followers. They have high interaction and deal with small-to-medium sized brands. High engagement rates are a result of their audience's faith in them. Additionally, they are typically easier to deal with and more engaged in their comments section due to having less followers than prominent influencers.

Micro influencers may be a fantastic place to start for a brand or company new to influencer marketing. Typically, they have a smaller budget than major influencers.

When working with micro influencers, there is typically a high level of brand exposure. Their audience is dedicated to following and seeing the influencer's posts, and they value their opinions, which may result in sales of the sponsored goods. This is typically observed with Instagram influencers who have been managing their account for a while—typically a few years.

Analyzing their engagement in comparison to a number of influencers with similar numbers of followers is another crucial piece of advice. You'll be able to determine their actual audience impact in this way. To ensure that the statistic is as current as feasible, this analysis has to be conducted on the influencer's most recent posts. An influencer marketing platform can help you locate and evaluate influencers quickly, and it can provide you with access to this and many other metrics.

Trend 5: Engagement and Community Building

Building a community that you can rely on in the far future (as a person or a brand) should be your top priority as a community manager, in my opinion. Although there are always tactics available online, including from us, my goal is to instill in you the understanding necessary to make the correct decisions and choose the appropriate inspiration, then tailor those strategies to the needs of your community. Because there isn't a one-size-fits-all solution, let's be honest. The ones I've tried that are the greatest for 2024 are even the ones I've listed.

Now, let's stop hesitating and explore how we can support one another in community development, which is and should be the main priority of most brands in 2024, if you agree with what I'm saying and want to learn more.

Why Are Community Building Strategies Important for Community Managers?

Assuming that you are already well-versed in community management and are simply looking for some strategic ideas for 2024, allow me to briefly discuss the benefits of having one. There is a very clear reason to do this. If you are not driven enough to see the benefits of having a community, you cannot create one.

Let's get right to it, then:

Community strategies guarantee that the objectives of your community are met by your efforts.

Good community-building techniques aid in drawing new members and keeping existing ones.

Allow yourself to concentrate on concepts that will genuinely benefit the society.

assists you in reevaluating the community's best practices that aren't currently working.

provides information on the opinions that consumers have about your brand.

allows for two-way conversation with your target audience, fostering long-lasting connections and more transparency.

These are a few of the crucial benefits that come with building a prosperous community in 2024. Furthermore, I think it's never too late to create or modify your plan if you agree with these benefits and wish your community to enjoy the same advantages.

The Value of Creating Virtual Communities

The following are the main justifications for why creating an online community is crucial in the current business environment:

Joint Social Action

Unexpected answers frequently arise from bringing people together in a community to discuss novel concepts or resolve problems. One of the main causes of the rising popularity of internal communities is this.

Conversely, if public communities are set up appropriately and enable you to find and interact with others in a way that is mutually beneficial, you can use them for collaboration. This can be applied to crowdsourcing or co-creation projects where participants collaborate to reach a common goal and feel included.

provide a better customer experience to set yourself apart from the competition.

Your organization can use online communities for internal goals such as content creation and marketing intelligence. However, consumers frequently contribute significantly to their overall happiness and experience. Even if your competitors and you might appear to be the same on paper, there could be big differences in an online community.

You may set yourself apart from the competition in an online member or customer community by responding to inquiries and offering surprises and joys either instantly or by developing products and services that satisfy your clients' needs.

Building Relationships

Community building gives you access to real human connections, something that SEO and other internet marketing strategies cannot match. Word-of-mouth marketing is the most reliable kind of advertising available to businesses. Today, businesses need to attract attention and build an audience—often referred to as a community—in order to thrive.

By doing this, you expose yourself to colleagues, influential people in the industry, people who will read and share your content, increasing the visibility of your company, as well as current and potential customers. Gaining those customers at a lower cost means that you are outperforming your rivals, exploring new markets and industry verticals, and—above all—building a much more robust enterprise.

Supplying information and acting as a reliable advisor.

Customers frequently look to the Internet for answers when they have queries or worries about services. Keywords from online consumer forums or communities pertaining to topics and content will show up in search results. Therefore, internet forums could be great resources for customers looking for answers to their research questions.

Paying attention

In your online community, you should listen just as much as you share when done correctly; in fact, there are situations when hearing more is ideal. This is a great approach to get opinions and understanding of the work your organization is performing at the moment. Actually, you will typically get feedback right away. If you can understand the needs, problems, and interests of your audience, you may change your entire business model.

As important as listening is, you also need to take prompt, constructive action with the knowledge you learn. It won't go over well to tell your customers they're wrong, but if you pay attention to what they have to say and implement some of their suggestions when they make sense, they'll feel valued.

The benefits of an online community much outweigh those of a conventional social network. By developing a sound strategy and plan of action, your organization can leverage the influence of both internal and external audiences to improve its operations and results.

Strategies for Creating Communities in 2024

Almost 85% of internet firms concur that communities have had a beneficial impact on their business, therefore here are some recent figures to help you acquire that validation. For various businesses, this effect may manifest itself in different ways. But once it's in place, that becomes an issue.

Allow me to assist you with a roadmap that community managers will require in order to establish, develop, and maintain vibrant online communities that benefit their members as well as the companies or causes they support by 2024.

Determine Your Purpose: Establish a mission statement or clear purpose for your community that speaks to the needs and interests of your intended audience.

Methodical Approach: You will, of course, need to outline the reasons for your community's early planning. The reasons it should exist practically. Thus, consider this: For whom are you creating the community?

- What does this do for the community?
- What are the long-range objectives?
- What is the mission statement?
- Who has contributed what?
- What general effects will that have?

Indeed, you must be truthful when answering these basic and essential questions. Because strong online communities are driven by a purpose "bigger than money," which contributes to their success.

Segment Your Audience

Strategy: To better meet the unique needs and preferences of each segment, break your audience up into smaller groups according to their demographics, interests, or habits.

Methodical Approach: These days, who doesn't enjoy personalized interactions with brands?

Sending the same targeted email to every prospective client is a thing of the past. Sending a single tone-deaf email can actually have the opposite impact these days. Customers may feel ignored and uncared for, and they may wonder if they are purchasing from the correct business. Therefore, the rule is to divide up your audience into groups according to distinct buyer personas so that they feel included in the community as a whole. This division can be carried out according to factors including age, way of life, geography, values, interests, and personality.

As an illustration: With its "Just Do It" campaign, Nike originally intended to appeal to serious athletes. However, as the company has developed over the years, it has adapted its strategy to reflect the needs of its community, with a focus on women and girls and their access to sports-related programs worldwide.

Select The Appropriate Platform Approach: Based on the tastes, habits, and objectives of your audience as well as the type of material you provide, choose the right platform or platforms to house your community.

Methodical Approach: In 2024, there won't be many opportunities for any community you start to flourish without the proper platforms. Thus, make sure your study is complete. Examine the particular dynamics of your community and learn about their favored modes of interaction. Which do they prefer, Facebook or LinkedIn? Do they favor discussion forums or chat rooms? In addition, take into account elements like analytics, user engagement features, support for various content formats, demographics, and moderating tools. Therefore, picking the appropriate platform lets you measure audience response and participation level in the most natural way possible, whether it's through Facebook groups, trending platforms like Discord, or industry-specific Slack channels.

For instance: For example, have a look at the E-commerce Executive Network LinkedIn group, which focuses on improving the customer journey to keep them coming back. Members of the group converse and exchange ideas for improving the same. You can see one exchange like this one.

Engage In Active Participation With Your Community Plan: Encourage regular participation in conversations and timely response to messages and comments to promote active engagement.

Practical Approach: If you don't stick with something, especially a community, you can never hope to grow or create it. It is difficult, I know. However, if you want your community to function, you will need to put in that effort. Share information about subjects that interest your community. It's a fantastic method to let them know you value and are aware of their needs.

Moreover, I'm confident that interactive materials like surveys, examinations, competitions, newsletters, etc. will draw readers in and motivate interaction. Furthermore, online community management solutions can assist you in maintaining consistent monitoring of them after they begin engaging at a high rate.

Implement Community-Driven Projects and Plans: Give the people in your community the tools they need to take charge of the things that interest and excite them.

Methodical Approach: Take community-driven efforts to advance the causes that the community is passionate about once you've established a community of devoted clients. Members of your community wouldn't be motivated to take the initiative for a worthy cause in the absence of a front stand. Creating forums or channels inside your community where members may suggest and vote on ideas for projects or campaigns is the easiest method to accomplish this. To encourage participation in cooperative projects among the members of your community, you can also plan in-person gatherings. Select moderators who can maintain member motivation by routinely updating members on the status and advancement of community-driven projects.

As an illustration, the community at Apple has extended its educational program, speeding up learning chances in over 600 localities worldwide to give people access to coding, creativity, and career opportunities.

Accept UGC To Give Them A Sense of Value: Invite community members to submit their own content, experiences, and viewpoints to promote user-generated content (UGC).

Methodical Approach: I think you can assess UGC's effect on a community if you already know how it affects them. It's one of the greatest methods to encourage community members to participate in challenges or contests. The best platforms for members to share their user-generated content

(UGC), which includes images, videos, narratives, and testimonials, are Twitter and Instagram. The most genuine and potent recommendation for your brand that makes community members into brand ambassadors is this one. They will gradually begin to feel more obliged to your brand and more involved, depending on how you respond to their initiative.

For instance: If you visit Starbucks' Instagram page, you'll find plenty of inspiration on how to use user-generated content to build a vibrant brand community. When the brand launches a new product or takes an initiative, they consistently involve their customers, influencers, etc.

Utilize Influencer Marketing Strategy: By working with people who are well-known and influential in your community or sector, you can use influencer marketing to spread the word about your brand and reach new audiences.

Practical Approach: I suggest creative collaborations as a way to strengthen your community-building efforts. Influencers can assist you in creating a positive reputation for your company through ongoing partnerships and general excitement about new initiatives. This will occur in addition to your target audience's broader reach. Therefore, establish a specialized program for brand ambassadors with individuals who share your enthusiasm and allow them to promote your business at events and on social media.

For instance, Gymshark relies heavily on content created by influencers to cultivate a devoted fan base within their community. Influencers and athletes who have been carefully chosen to represent the brand will share their stories and spread the word, encouraging others who share their ambitions to become involved.

Co-Create Community Related Content Strategy: Give your community members a sense of ownership and involvement by involving them in the content production process and encouraging them to develop and generate community-related material.

Practical Approach: Co-creation is preferable to content creation for brand promotion, even if content creation is always possible. Let's just say that there are things you don't know. You should take advantage of this chance to engage your community and produce a lot of material. The amount of time and resources required will be greatly reduced, and you'll have access to relatable content that will improve customer engagement. It's easy to understand why. Community-based creators and influencers are more familiar with the tastes and demographics of the grassroots. In order to produce a variety of material, such as social media posts, flat lays, product-only photos, films, and so forth, you can collaborate with them.

As an illustration, consider Sephora and its Beauty Insider Community, which provides a forum for members to exchange beauty advice and collaborate on content creation in an effort to attract a new generation of beauty fans to the company.

Organize Exclusive Live Or In-Person Events: Organize exclusive live events to give your community members engaging and different experiences.

Methodical Approach: There's nothing quite like the appeal of special live or in-person events—after all, who doesn't want to have a little fun? The objective is to personally design and coordinate live events for your community members only, such as webinars, workshops, masterclasses, Q&A sessions, pop-up stores, virtual meetups, or in-person gatherings. Therefore, you may build the stronger community you want to see faster if you are ready to take your actions offline.

For instance: For example, as part of their community-building efforts, Rainbow Room invited its devoted fans to an in-person pop-up tiki bar event, providing them with a more relaxed environment with snacks, drinks, and cocktails.

Provide Rewards And Express Recognition For Contributions

Technique: Promote involvement and interaction in your community by rewarding members for their contributions and providing incentives.

Methodical Approach: Community involvement, in my opinion, always benefits both parties, and you should thank or honor the community's members for their enormous commitment and contribution. They will feel inspired and driven to continue participating and being dedicated when they receive appreciation and acknowledgment, which goes a long way.

You may provide them with rewards like:

- special benefits
- Discount Coupons for Rewards
- Invitations to free events
- badges and community awards
- Courses offering free instruction
- Cards as gifts
- Free Goods
- Freebies, gifts, etc.

Just make sure the prizes are in line with the goals of your business and the desires of the people in your community.

As an illustration, Adidas has a fantastic approach to community development since it provides a fantastic rewards system to increase adiClub member involvement. Benefits like early bird access to basic activities, discount codes, and exclusive deals may be available to members. This is an excellent long-term engagement strategy.

Promote Interactions With Other Communities

Method: Encourage cross-promotion with other communities that have similar audiences or interests to broaden your reach and foster collaboration.

Methodical Approach: Finally, this is a tactic that I wholeheartedly endorse. Finding organizations or communities in your sector or niche that complement your brand and community values is all it takes to achieve it. Just get in touch with them to find out what interests them. Find out if they are open to discussing joint ventures, such as guest blogging, social media takeovers, co-hosting events, contests, challenges, or sweepstakes. Work together on campaigns or promotions, and make sure the result benefits the community's members as well. In this sense, it creates chances in the future to focus on new markets and demographics.

For instance: If you are unaware, let me tell you about the well-known partnership between Apple and Nike. They have worked together to offer their community members and customers a new product experience. Together, they were able to produce the Nike Watch, which both businesses assert works with the Nike Run Club app. For runners, this product is fantastic. This product is available on the official websites of Nike and Apple.

User-Generated Content and Advocacy within Communities

The burgeoning field of digital marketing, where authenticity is paramount, has witnessed a remarkable surge in the popularity of User Generated Content (UGC). Imagine a vast group of brand lovers willingly producing material that not only extols the virtues of the brand but also speaks to its essence. Welcome to the modern era of marketing, where creating experiences is just as important as promoting messages. Fast-forward through the what, why, and how of user-generated content, which is the key to success for brands trying to attract, interest, and convert customers.

Comprehending the Fundamentals: User Generated Content: What Is It?

User Generated Content is the digital equivalent of the conductor giving up the baton and letting the audience sing solo. It's material produced by users, fans, or customers that highlights their thoughts, feelings, or experiences with a company or item. User Generated Content (UGC) is the real voice of the people in the digital world, ranging from tweets and blog mentions to Instagram posts and YouTube reviews.

Here's Why UGC Will Be Needed in 2024: 1. Well, the secret is authenticity.

UGC exudes genuineness. It's actual people sharing real stories, not some well-written advertisement material. And what do you know? Customers of today are drawn to genuineness. Consumer suggestions are more credible than any carefully produced advertisement.

2. Establishing Credibility, Post by Post

Nothing fosters trust more than having satisfied customers spread the word about you. Because user-generated material is objective, sincere, and personable, potential customers are more inclined to believe it.

3. Expanding Participation and Audience

UGC attracts interaction like a magnet. People are inspired when they witness their friends utilizing and adoring your stuff. UGC also has the amazing potential to go viral, greatly extending the reach of your business beyond what can be accomplished with conventional marketing techniques.

4. Putting Gas in Your Content Engine

Are you having trouble coming up with new content? UGC resembles a bottomless pit. UGC can be recycled for use in blog entries, social media postings, or even your upcoming advertising campaign. It maintains your material varied, current, and fresh.

Here it is: a thorough guide to maximizing user-generated content in 2024.

Your brand may build a genuine and interesting relationship with your audience by being aware of its subtleties, supporting different kinds of content, and adhering to best practices.

The Influence of Community Development and Authenticity

Authenticity is the magic wand that turns mistrust into trust at a time when people are wary of traditional marketing. UGC is authenticity personified. Users who willingly share their experiences lend legitimacy to the conversation. User-generated content (UGC) is a powerful tool for establishing brand trust since people trust peer recommendations more than well-produced commercials.

Data and Statistics: Unveiling the UGC Phenomenon

Now let's examine some striking figures that highlight the importance of User Generated Content in the digital environment:

Influence on purchasing Decisions: Ninety percent of consumers say user-generated content (UGC) influences their purchasing decisions, per a TurnTo Networks survey. Genuine experiences from other customers have a greater impact than well chosen brand messaging.

2. Effect on Social Media Engagement: User-generated content (UGC) drives social media platforms. Posts on Instagram featuring UGC have a 4.5% higher conversion rate than other post kinds. It's about turning participation into action, not simply about likes.

3. Trust-Building Dynamics: According to a Stackla customer survey, 86% of respondents think that authenticity matters when choosing which brands to like and support. Since UGC exudes genuineness, it acts as a strong magnet for brand attachment.

4. Diversity and Originality of material: Companies that use user-generated material gain from a wide range of content. User-generated content (UGC) infuses creativity into the brand narrative, making it approachable and lively. This includes reviews, testimonials, images, and videos.

The Profit-Return Explosion: Making Gold Out of User Content

The debate isn't only about how popular UGC is; it's also about how much of an impact it may have financially on your brand.

1. Skyrocketing Conversion Rates: A Yotpo study found that visitors who engage with user-generated content have a 97% higher chance of converting than non-interactive users. User-generated content's genuine quality converts browsers into consumers.

2. Increasing E-Commerce Sales: UGC is a sales-boosting tactic, not merely a feel-good one. According to Bazaarvoice, showing reviews on an online store can result in a 270% increase in conversion rates.

3. Cost-Effective Content development: User-generated content (UGC) turns your audience into content providers, saving you money on traditional content development. It's an economical tactic without sacrificing quality.

4. Mastery of Social Media Marketing: UGC campaigns have an average engagement rate on social media that is 28% greater than that of typical brand posts. It's about active participation that converts into return on investment rather than just visibility.

Brands Mastering the UGC Game: Exemplary Case Studies

1. Starbucks: Crafting Communal Bonds

The #RedCupContest from Starbucks is a fantastic illustration of UGC genius. Starbucks invites patrons to post pictures of their festive red cups on social media every holiday season. What was the outcome? a tsunami of user-generated content that builds excitement for the holidays and fosters a sense of community while simultaneously promoting Starbucks. It's a shared experience, not simply coffee.

2. GoPro: Taking the UGC Trend by Storm

By encouraging its users to share the adventurous experiences they have using GoPro cameras, GoPro has transformed its clientele into brand advocates. The #GoPro hashtag highlights the items' versatility and is a veritable gold mine of breathtaking content. It's a ticket to adventure, not just a camera.

3. Adobe: Honoring Creative Prowess

Adobe's #AdobeStock360 campaign is proof of UGC's effectiveness in the business-to-business market. By encouraging consumers to use Adobe Stock materials to demonstrate their creativity, they transformed their products into instruments for creative expression. It's a canvas for imaginative minds, not just software.

Choosing Your UGC Approach A Harmony of Personality and Professionalism Now that we've discovered the power of user-generated content, let's dive into how you can use it into your marketing plan while maintaining professionalism and uniqueness. Set Explicit Rules Promote UGC while establishing explicit rules. Inform your tribe about the kinds of content that suit your brand. Communicate in a straightforward but cordial manner, creating an atmosphere of cooperation rather than authority.

2. generate embedded Use of hashtags Hardcoded hashtags are UGC campaigns' eyeblink. Create a hashtag that captures the essence of your business, is memorable, and is simple to spell. Add a little uniqueness to make it memorable and viral. 3. have an impact on UGC across platforms UGC is not restricted to a single medium. Share the love on your website, in your marketing materials, and on social media. Make sure the content you choose for your brand is professionally curated and fits your look. 4. Involve and Recognize Admit stoners' contributions to UGC and interact with them. Expressing gratitude can be quite beneficial. Include a little of your brand voice in your answers to convey warmth and gratitude.

Best Practices to Remember

1. Always ask for permission Prior to employing user-generated content (UGC) in your marketing collateral, always get permission. It guarantees that you adhere to moral and legal bounds in addition to being dutiful.

2. Give Proper Credit to the Original Author Give due credit to the original creator when using user-generated content (UGC). Acknowledging the contributor of a video or social media post improves your rapport with your audience.

3. Adopt Transparency Indicate with ease when material has been created by users. Translucence promotes trust by demonstrating that you respect the thoughts and experiences of your visitors.

4. Moderation is essential In addition to being real, content must be moderated to make sure it adheres to your brand's principles and values. To keep your brand's reputation intact, uphold explicit temperance principles.

UGC—Your Brand's Best Kept Secret In the complex world of digital marketing, user-generated content becomes more than just a tactic—it becomes a revolutionary force. It serves as a bridge between brands and their fan base, transforming marketing into a cooperative endeavor. Brands are rewriting the laws of interaction by using the authenticity and inventiveness of their fanbase, from Starbucks to GoPro. Thus, whether you're using Adobe Flash Reverse to release your creative side or beginning on a Starbucks cappuccino, a GoPro, or other camera, Your brand is more than simply a product—it's a narrative that needs to be shared. Allow user-generated content to be the professional and charming pen that writes it. Because in the realm of user-generated content (UGC), each click, share, and hashtag is a new chapter in the success story of your brand.

Trend 6: Ephemeral Content and Storytelling

The majority of social media marketers are fully aware that social media material is always changing. Content that is available for a brief period of time before disappearing is known as ephemeral content, and it is one of the most fascinating and widely used evolutions. (For example, consider Instagram Stories or Snapchat Stories.)

Although investing in ephemeral content tactics can seem paradoxical due to its transient nature, done well, they can provide distinct advantages in the congested digital world. Photo or video content that is automatically destroyed shortly after it is submitted is referred to as ephemeral content. Users can share images or posts on apps such as Instagram Stories and Snapchat that are only visible for a day before they vanish.

Ephemeral material can be shared publicly or sent to specific people or groups. It can include everything from narrative tales and live-streamed videos to product demos and behind-the-scenes footage.

Why does ephemeral work so well to increase attention and engagement?

It offers users a fresh approach to producing original content. Ephemeral content is an efficient approach to produce engaging material at a low cost, making it useful for advertisers as well as casual Instagram or Snapchat users.

Platforms that support transient content are designed to support vertical video playback, which is advantageous given that 94% of smartphone users hold their devices vertically and never bother to turn their screens sideways for optimal viewing.

Because of the casual and low-cost setup, ephemeral content appears more genuine, personal, and impromptu. It allows you to communicate brand messages to followers and provide value without coming across as overly promotional.

It's entertaining — Snapchat and Instagram are well-known for their distinctive in-built filters, stickers, voice overs, and brand integrations that enhance the experience of creating and/or using the app.

It makes use of people's fear of missing out on things on social media (FOMO). People are encouraged to interact with the content before it expires because it only lasts for a day. Because of this, traffic from ephemeral content is generated by the surge in views and engagement that coincides with the publication of new material.

It assists in avoiding oversharing, which can lead to a decline in followers and engagement. Ephemeral material is published on Stories rather than the main feed, so your followers won't be inundated with postings in a single day in addition to its brief lifespan.

Social media content types that are transient

Let's take a quick look at the various categories of transient content seen on social media platforms:

Stories on Instagram

Instagram Stories are images or videos that disappear after a whole day. Numerous interactive components are included, including polls, question areas, stickers, and links. Your stories can be preserved in Story Highlights so they will remain accessible even after they are removed from your feed.

Narratives have the potential to generate leads and sales. A research found that 43% of social media users watch Instagram Stories more frequently than other forms of video content.

Stories on Facebook

Like Instagram Stories, Facebook Stories appear on your feed for a single day. Users can add text, stickers, and filters to their posts using these, which are showcased at the top of the newsfeed. Friends, followers, or a user-specified custom audience can view Facebook stories.

Stories on Snapchat

A compilation of "snaps" taken throughout the last 24 hours makes up a Snapchat story. Your stories can live longer if you store them in Memories. They could be a lot of fun to use to record and share your brand's actions with your audience.

Stories on TikTok

Videos on TikTok that remain on your feed for a full day are called TikTok stories, or TikTok moments. Links, hashtags, other accounts can be tagged, and location tags can be added. TikTok stories are made exclusively through momentous content capture, in contrast to Instagram Stories.

To learn more about social media stories and some of the best ways to utilize its capabilities, read this blog.

Telling Stories to Engage People with Your Brand.

There's nothing like hearing or reading a compelling story. This is why films, television series, and novels are so popular. When we immerse ourselves in a story, emotions flow, characters come to life, and our imaginations go wild. It's fun. It's intriguing. It's magical.

And there's science behind it. Our brains are hardwired to interact with stories. Brain chemicals such as dopamine, oxytocin, and endorphins form emotional connections, causing us to care about the story's outcome and keep listening, reading, or watching until the finish.

So, can you imagine what would happen if you integrated stories into your brand's content?

You can increase trust, engage your audience, and develop solid relationships.

In fact, research suggests that storytelling can increase brand connection and trust by 4% while influencing 68% of buyers' purchasing decisions.

This section delves into ways for creating narratives that resonate with viewers.

Stand out from the pack and fascinate your audience with these brand storytelling tactics.

1. Create clear and engaging narratives.

Narratives that connect with your audience and create lasting memories are an excellent method to raise brand awareness and recognition.

But it all boils down to telling straightforward stories that anybody can understand and relate to.

Before sharing your story, make sure you are acquainted with your audience. Understand their preferences, interests, and level of competence on the issue.

Otherwise, your story may confuse them. Improve clarity by:

Use detailed language and vivid facts to generate clear images in the audience's minds, rather than simply telling them.

To keep the plot flowing, make smooth transitions between sections of your narrative.

Make sure that the message or takeaway you want your audience to understand is as clear as possible.

Using visuals, such as photos, charts, or graphs, to improve comprehension and recall.

Maintain a consistent tone, brand voice, style, and perspective throughout your tale.

Create a clear structure for your story, including a beginning, middle, and end.

Using clear and straightforward wording.

A simple and easy-to-understand story captivates and helps you connect with your audience more effectively.

That's where tools like an online paraphraser come in handy, allowing you to effortlessly rearrange your message - especially if you have a large writing team with a variety of styles.

Improving consistency and comprehension leads to higher engagement levels.

2. Use humor.

Use comedy to make your story more engaging and pleasant. The phrase "laughter is the best medicine" is true, especially when it comes to storytelling.

Combining the satisfaction people get from hearing an inspiring narrative with laughing results in a powerful encounter that leaves a lasting impression on your audience.

Humor might also help your audience feel more at ease.

For example, the project management application ClickUp incorporates humor into its social media material, especially on platforms like Instagram and TikTok, where visually appealing videos do well. This famous video tries to remove the stigma associated with project management, making the topic more approachable and interesting.

The brand additionally communicates with its target demographic with comparable content (which is also popular). This method promotes a sense of connection and understanding.

In summary, a personal narrative style establishes an emotional connection with viewers and fosters trust in the business.

3. Share Customers' Success Stories

Reviews and testimonials are effective tools for brand storytelling, providing narratives that audiences can connect with on a personal level.

They're also likely to recall these customer anecdotes.

Need proof? Stories have a 12 times greater impact than facts alone.

Sure, it's always a good idea to talk about how great your product or service is, and to give data about how you can assist your clients improve their lives.

However, when you publish success stories from previous customers, you add social proof, demonstrating to leads and prospects that they, too, can achieve the same results if they give your company a chance.

Tailor Brands, a forerunner in the field of assisting budding entrepreneurs in starting a firm, has expertly used the power of reviews to create a captivating narrative that goes beyond typical marketing methods.

Reviews, whether on platforms like Trustpilot or customer testimonials on Tailor Brands' website, provide genuine anecdotes from real customers.

The organization offers a unique view into the customer experience, providing insights that go beyond product features.

Each review becomes a chapter in the brand's story, describing how customers have found value and success through Tailor Brands' services.

Form Health, an online medical weight loss clinic, is another brand that takes advantage of consumer testimonials. The brand told the narrative of Shelbie, who comes from an Italian family whose gatherings are typically centered around food.

From there, Shelbie describes her experience with Form Health and recalls warmly her first conversation with her nutritionist, Vicki.

She discusses the valuable things she has gained on her path. But it's more than just what she says.

It also includes the events she recounts with her family and cuisine, as well as how she discusses her experiences. This enhances our imagination and keeps us engaged.

4. Create Curiosity and Intrigue to Capture Your Audience's Attention.

Create a great hook to capture your audience's attention. A good hook is a very powerful pop culture approach because it makes listeners want to see the story unfold.

For example, the popular TV program Breaking Bad opens with a high-intensity, action-packed sequence in which the main character, Walter White, drives an RV through the desert.

He's dressed only in his underwear and a gas mask, creating an intriguing opening tableau that keeps the spectator guessing about what's going on. This moment exemplifies superb storytelling.

You don't need to create a spectacular beginning hook, but you can learn from its execution to pique your audience's interest and keep them engaged.

For example, you might begin your story with a gripping hook or ask an intriguing question to immediately capture your audience's attention

5. Don't be afraid to be creative.

Every narrative you tell does not need to be factual.

It makes no difference if your stories are reality or fiction as long as they are relevant to your business and industry and interest your audience in some way.

So don't think you can't be innovative; you surely can.

Assume you're a courier service operator that offers same-day deliveries.

During the holidays, buyers frequently worry about their packages arriving in time for Christmas. You can make a delightful story about Santa Claus and his elves.

The story might depict how the elves have collaborated with different delivery drivers and how the reindeer vans are equipped to complete all deliveries on the same day or night.

6. Connect with Your Audience Through Empathy and Emotion

What if you wish to educate your audience on a specific notion or idea? However, you must do so in an engaging manner.

It might be tough to convey a complex issue like student loan refinancing.

Consider the emotional and financial effects student loans have on students and young professionals to guarantee your message is received effectively.

This includes examining the complexity of refinancing, acknowledging the stress it causes, and analyzing the benefits and opportunities it might provide.

As a result, you can turn your narrative into an effective instrument for engaging, educating, and supporting your audience.

7. Increase Authenticity by Sharing Your Brand's History.

Your brand is more than just a business. Real people developed and controlled this entity.

As a result, it is critical to convey this in all of your communications. You can accomplish this by explaining how everything began.

Why did you wish to start your own business? What was the motivation behind it all?

By sharing these intriguing stories, you appear genuine and personable.

So, why not talk about the individuals behind it, what motivates them, and how they came up with their business idea?

People enjoy engaging with (and purchasing from) some brands due to their openness. People enjoy getting to know the faces behind the brands. That is why StoryChief emphasizes its core team on the About Us page.

Additionally, it promotes long-term consumer relationships and loyalty.

8. Promote Narrative-Driven Content on Social Media.

Social media offers an excellent chance for brand storytelling.

Many consumers use social media to find product ideas, read news updates, and keep up with influencers and celebrities. However, the primary motivation for using social media is to connect with others.

This includes connecting with brands, as 90% of consumers follow at least one on social media.

Engage your audience by offering client testimonials, personal stories about how you overcome a challenge, or introducing brand stories about the roots of your company.

Post captivating captions and incorporate your brand personality into your postings to develop strong connections with your audience.

Crafting compelling captions for social media has become easier in the age of AI, with tools like an AI caption generator making the process simpler.

These solutions simplify caption production and allow for easy modification, allowing marketers to adapt their tales and connect authentically with their target audience.

9. Use metaphors to convey technical concepts.

When people hear metaphors, they frequently experience a sense of familiarity. This is useful for explaining a complex topic or concept.

As you employ metaphors in your narrative, your viewers will begin to comprehend that, despite their lack of familiarity with the topic, what you're elaborating on is something they already know.

For instance, if the subject is adopting new technology, discuss how it's comparable to completing a marathon.

It demands rigorous planning, a steady pace, and a strong dedication. And the finish line is not the end, but rather a transition to the next phase.

10. Evaluate the success of your storytelling efforts.

It's time to assess the effectiveness of your narrative strategy after putting the aforementioned tactics into practice.

In order to evaluate how your storytelling affects audience engagement, think about utilizing a session replay tool.

Why brands may benefit from ephemeral content

Ephemeral content is being used by a lot of brands across various mediums. Is it because they're simpler to make, or do they help the brand achieve its marketing objectives? Both of them are!

Images and short-form films increase interaction.

In a world where people enjoy shorter material, ephemeral content is ideal.

Sprout's Content Benchmarks Report indicates that the most engaging kind of in-feed content is short-form video content, which generally works well for companies. Because stories are short and contain interactive aspects, we may confidently conclude that this also applies to them.

Stories with short-form content can encourage impulsive purchases or signups. or to rapidly establish a connection and provide updates to your audience. By establishing regular, low-lift touchpoints with your audience, ephemeral content can help you stay relevant in their minds and boost brand awareness.

Uses FOMO to draw in viewers

One of the biggest draws of deciduous material for marketers and content providers is the miracle known as FOMO, or fear of missing out. Since your followers are apprehensive that they only have a brief window of time to examine the content, there's a sense of urgency. Let's say you would like to ask questions on the weekend and your favored brand answers questions from the general public.

You wouldn't want to pass up this chance. In an analogous tone, you may employ time-sensitive conditioning to induce interest and engagement in your brand. Stories are a common tool used by numerous businesses to showcase their rearmost product launches and unique offers. Little bits of the content are being published, which heightens the sense of urgency and engagement.

It improves sincerity

Social media druggies prefer" real- life" brand material. Sow Social conducted a study and set up that 64 of consumers stated they seek a connection to a brand. deciduous content allows you to showcase the mortal side of your brand on social media by using" in the moment" footage. This makes your content and brand more relatable and individualized because it's unscripted and not exorbitantly edited. You might make a near connection with your target followership by releasing exclusive or behind- the- scenes content.

It's further garrulous

While in- feed content is primarily concerned with growing your followership, deciduous content is intended to be participated with your followers. utmost platforms give a variety of interactive features that are unique to temporary media. These can take the form of asking questions, carrying out checks, or putting out specific calls to action. Brands may simply use these chops to get the types of relations they want from their followership, whether their thing is to increase deals or brand visibility.

Another reason for its lesser engagement is the" low pressure" of deciduous information. Because the content is limited in duration, druggies do not have to second- guess their response when interacting with it. People who are too backward to note on a post or direct communication might be more likely to interact because their response is not incontinently recorded in the in- feed information.

Creating Witching Narratives to Promote Brand Relinquishment

Brands need to stand out further than ever in the congested request of the moment. Developing absorbing brand tales is one approach to achieve this. An explanation of a brand's origins, principles, and objects is handed by its brand story. It's a system of erecting emotional connections with guests in order to win their trust and fidelity.

A well- drafted brand story has the implicit to be an important marketing tool. It could be useful to you Boost the mindfulness of your brand. Boost customer commerce Boost the fidelity of your guests. produce a more important brand identity. So, how can one develop an engaging brand narrative? Then some pointers make a solid foundation first. The story of your brand should be erected around its charge and abecedarian values.

Which beliefs do you hold?

What pretensions are you trying to achieve? You can start casting your story after you've laid the base. Keep effects easy. Your brand narrative needs to be easy to comprehend and recall. Steer clear of specialized language and slang. Rather, concentrate on chronicling an accessible and brief story to your followership. Be true to yourself. The narrative behind your brand needs to be real and credible. no way try to pass for someone you are not. Communicate openly about the pretensions, values, and background of your brand.

Make use of feeling

Stories that arouse feelings in people are more likely to connect with them. Make use of your narrative to appeal to the solicitations, fears, expedients, and dreams of your followership. Be material. Your target followership should be suitable to relate to your brand story. What kinds of effects intrigue them? Which areas hurt them the most? ensure that your tale resonates with them on a particular position.

Tell it constantly. Do not just partake in the backstory of your brand formerly and move on. Partake it on social media, your website, and promotional accoutrements. People are more likely to identify with your brand the further times they hear your narrative. Then are a many cases of companies that have successfully conveyed witching

Nike Inspiration and provocation are crucial to the brand's narrative. The pot regularly uses athletes who overcome rigors to come extremely successful in its advertising. Those that aspire to negotiate their own pretensions can relate to this narrative. Apple's brand narrative is centered on design and invention. The company's advertisements contain imaginative and eye-catching imagery, and its products are frequently seen as status symbols. Those who appreciate complication and style will find this novel appealing.

Starbucks Connection and community are crucial to the brand's narrative. workers are encouraged to get to know their guests as the pot wants its stores to be friendly and cozy. People who are looking for a place to relax and mingle will find this story to be applicable.

These are just a many cases of how using brand liars can strengthen your brand and help you connect with consumers. Making an engaging brand narrative that appeals to your target request is a commodity you should consider if you want to grow your company.

- Then there are many further pointers for casting an engaging brand narrative.
- When telling your story,
- use pictorial imagery and illustrations.
- Make your narrative relatable and unique.

- Arouse your followership's feelings with humor or other prayers.
- Keep your story's voice and tone harmonious with your brand.
- Get input from other people to make sure your narrative is brief and accessible.

Although it takes time and work to produce an engaging brand story, the prices are great. It can be a useful tool for creating a successful brand if done right.

How Your Marketing Strategy Can Include Ephemeral Content

Despite the fact that ephemeral content is more impromptu than other kinds of content, planning beforehand is still advised.

The same three essential stages that apply to other forms of content also apply to ephemeral content: identify objectives, produce content, and track outcomes. Understand your audience first, though.

Be aware of your audience.

Determine first the level of motivation and the best times for your target audience to watch and interact with fading material. A social media management platform like Sprout or native analytics can be used to ascertain this.

Your ephemeral strategy can be improved, for instance, if your Instagram Story has a bigger daily unique reach.

Clarify your objectives.

Once you are aware of the interest your audience has in short-lived content, make goals that align with the production of such material. Ephemeral material can help achieve the following common goals:

- Boost the exposure of your brand.
- Expand the size of your email list.
- Get prompt feedback on goods and services.
- Encourage them to visit other websites, such blogs.
- Make sales
- Choose the formats for your work.

Try your hand at creating transient content without fear. Here are a few concepts you can use:

- An insider's perspective
- entertaining surveys
- client endorsements and success narratives.
- Features and uses for your product Q&A sessions with a specialist.

Think about making some of your current material temporary to start. You can make brief, captivating snippets, for instance, by using the highlights from a recently released podcast episode.

Ensure that your plan for ephemeral material incorporates storytelling. The intended outcomes are unlikely to be achieved by a compilation of disconnected content elements.

As an alternative, you can use ephemeral content as a means of assessing audience interest in content you plan to produce in the future. Assume you wish to produce a YouTube video on a particular subject. How can a topic with transient substance be thoroughly examined? You may use a poll to directly ask your audience about engagement, or you may use vanishing content on the subject to measure engagement.

When the time comes to distribute the material, think about how frequently you ought to release ephemeral content. This will change based on the intended audience and platform. To locate the ideal times to publish for your target audience, you can use Sprout Social's viral post technology or analyze the metrics on your social media platforms.

Moreover, schedule and publish Instagram stories and other kinds of content in advance with a scheduling tool like Sprout.

Monitor the effectiveness of the content.

Observe the performance to find out what kind of transient content works best for your audience. It is crucial to keep an eye on how each piece of transient material you publish is performing. Seek to determine how to enhance its functionality. Observe the following information:

What kind of temporary material attracted the greatest attention, comments, and engagement?

When are users most likely to interact with it?

How are they directing traffic?

How do they impact after engagement?

To find themes or phrases that speak to your target audience, do a qualitative investigation. The websites listed below can assist you in learning more about social media result tracking.

Trend 7: Social Commerce

The merging of social networking and online buying has created a potent phenomena known as social commerce in the quickly evolving e-commerce market. In 2024, social networking platforms and e-commerce will be more integrated than ever before, offering businesses previously unheard-of chances for expansion and client interaction. This guide will walk you through the ever-changing landscape of social commerce and offer insights into how companies may best take use of its potential to increase sales, foster customer loyalty, and outperform rivals.

Moreover, it is evident that by 2024, the e-commerce and social media sectors would experience substantial changes. Social commerce—the merging of social media and online shopping—has the potential to completely change how we engage with brands and make purchases. In this change, TikTok Shop has become a major player, indicating that social commerce will eventually become the primary driver.

The Explosion of TikTok Stores and Revenue Paths
The emergence of TikTok Shop signifies a momentous change in the e-commerce terrain. The platform is being used more and more by brands and creators to connect and engage with customers. This creates a whole new revenue stream and offers influencers and content producers a special chance to easily include commerce into their work.

Platform Distinctiveness and Growing Audience In 2024, social media platforms understand that in order to retain and expand their user base, it's critical to embrace their distinctive qualities. For navigating individuals' varied tastes and behaviors across many platforms, this specialized approach is essential. An essential component of social media strategy will be identifying the distinct goals of each channel.

Making Use of Special Features and Customization The revival of the Threads app is one noteworthy trend that suggests a renewed focus on developing genuine, real connections on social media. This focus on customization aligns with the increasing trend of brands using creator content as adverts, taking advantage of influencer-generated content's true appeal and engagement potential.

AI Integration and Revenue Prospects for Creators
AI is anticipated to be a key component in simplifying workflows and creating new revenue streams for creators in the dynamic social media landscape. AI's ability to open up new revenue streams is an intriguing possibility that meshes nicely with the general theme of 2024's social media trends.

The Confluence of E-Commerce and Social Media
Social media and e-commerce coming together is changing the way companies engage with their clients and spurring new ideas and approaches to marketing. In 2024, social media engagement and consumer decision-making are predicted to see a rebirth thanks to platforms like TikTok spearheading the social commerce movement.

The rise of social media platforms for commerce

In 2024, social commerce will become a vital field for marketers operating at an eCommerce and social media intersection. The vital data, patterns, and strategies that marketers need to thrive in this interconnected environment are provided in this guide.

We'll discuss success stories and examine how social commerce is changing sales and customer involvement. Get ready to change your approach after reading our comprehensive analysis of the social commerce landscape.

Social commerce: what is it?

Social commerce is the revolutionary combination of social media with e-commerce that creates a virtual environment where purchasing is easily incorporated into everyday social interactions. With the help of this creative concept, people can easily move from browsing to buying on their preferred social networks.

Market volume and forecasts

Social commerce is predicted to reach a startling US $1.95 trillion market size by 2026, demonstrating the industry's remarkable financial trajectory. With a prognosis that shows a surge above US $6 trillion by 2030, it is clear that customer preference is shifting toward social media as a focus for shopping.

eCommerce Companies and Customer Interaction Forward-thinking eCommerce companies are taking advantage of social commerce's potential to connect with a sizable and engaged user base. This calculated action aims to integrate businesses into consumers' everyday life and create a more meaningful, deeper relationship than typical online purchasing experiences. It is not simply about increasing revenue.

Why is social commerce so crucial?

With more than 4.5 billion people using social media globally, social commerce is expanding more quickly than traditional eCommerce, which suggests that consumers are shifting their spending habits to include integrated social experiences.

Since Millennials and Gen Z mostly rely on social media for inspiration and transactions, influencers are extremely important in influencing their buying decisions. This change impacts not just the way consumers shop, but also the places and people they trust, which is why social commerce is a key area of attention for contemporary e-commerce tactics.

Recognizing the Effects of Social Media on E-Commerce

Social media has completely changed how customers communicate with companies and make purchases. The development and success of e-commerce enterprises have been greatly impacted by the emergence of social media platforms. This section will examine how social commerce fits into contemporary retail and the ways that interactive shopping trends have changed how people connect with brands.

Trends in Interactive Shopping: Passive to Active Consumer Engagement.

Consumers no longer passively browse online catalogs. The evolution of interactive shopping has allowed consumers to actively participate in the purchasing process. Social media platforms now include shoppable posts, interactive videos, and augmented reality (AR) applications that improve the shopping experience and allow customers to see products in their own environments.

With these interactive elements, customers can actively participate in the decision-making process, increasing satisfaction and the likelihood of making a purchase.

Table: Impact of Social Media on E-Commerce and Consumer Engagement

Impact	Description
Increased Reach	Social media platforms provide a vast audience reach, enabling businesses to connect with a larger and more diverse customer base.
Enhanced Brand Awareness	By leveraging social media marketing strategies, businesses can increase their brand visibility and recognition among social media users.
Improved Customer Engagement	Interactive features offered by social media platforms allow for active consumer engagement, fostering a deeper connection between brands and customers.
Personalized	Social media algorithms

Recommendations	can analyze user data and preferences to deliver personalized product recommendations, improving the shopping experience for consumers.
User-Generated Content (UGC) Impact	Consumers can share their experiences and opinions about products through user-generated content, influencing purchasing decisions and building trust.
Accelerated Buying Process	With the integration of social commerce features, consumers can seamlessly transition from discovery to purchase, reducing friction in the buying process.

Social media's influence on e-commerce and customer involvement will only grow as the digital landscape changes. In the dynamic world of e-commerce, brands who adopt these trends and actively interact with their clientele on social media will have a competitive edge.

Integrating social networks and e-commerce platforms is the evolution of shopping.

Social networks and e-commerce platforms are becoming less distinct, giving marketers more ways to interact with consumers. It makes sense that social media, with its continued dominance over our daily lives, would have a big influence on our purchasing habits. We'll examine how social media and e-commerce platforms have changed the way people shop today, as well as the fascinating developments that are reshaping the retail industry.

Shopping via livestream is becoming more and more popular.

Livestream shopping has become a revolutionary trend in the e-commerce market in recent years. This innovative idea adds the thrill of in-the-moment video contact to the buying experience. Customers may interact with their favorite companies and influencers while seeing product demos, asking questions, and making purchases straight from the livestream.

Watch Live Buying

The popularity of livestream purchasing has increased since it can authentically and urgently communicate a sense of urgency. By showcasing their products in use and offering prompt feedback, brands can foster consumer confidence and establish trust. Livestreaming has the ability to transform the way we shop and the e-commerce industry thanks to the power of social media platforms.

Augmented Reality Integration with Social Media Promotion

The usage of augmented reality (AR) in social media marketing is one of the most fascinating innovations. By allowing consumers to superimpose digital items on the real world, augmented reality technology enhances the interaction and personalization of the shopping experience.

Companies can employ augmented reality to give consumers virtual try-on experiences so they can see how items will fit or appear before they buy. With the help of their smartphones or other augmented reality (AR)-enabled devices, users can virtually apply makeup or try on garments in the beauty and fashion industries.

Augmented reality is being used in social media marketing to boost engagement and give brands useful data. By examining user interactions and preferences, businesses can acquire valuable insights into consumer behavior and adjust their marketing campaigns accordingly. Augmented reality (AR) has the power to change the way businesses engage with their consumers and produce immersive experiences that boost revenue.

Social media and e-commerce platforms are coming together, livestreaming is becoming more popular, and augmented reality is being used more and more, all of which have given firms new chances to meaningfully engage with customers. To fully benefit from social media in e-commerce, firms need to keep up with the newest trends and modify their marketing strategy in line with technological advancements.

The advantages of social commerce

1. A wider audience base.

Social networking is a popular place for Generation Z and Millennials to shop.

Due to their preference for digital platforms, Millennials and Generation Z are increasingly making social media their main online shopping destination. Because these individuals utilize social media frequently, they make excellent targets for social commerce campaigns.

On social media, there are a lot of possible clients.

Social commerce has a huge potential customer base because social media is used by billions of people. Companies can expand into new markets by utilizing this enormous audience.

expanding the group of people you want to reach.

Social media's worldwide reach allows firms to connect with consumers anywhere in the world. Growth depends on this development, particularly when more people across a range of demographics start using social shopping.

2. A seamless experience when buying.

Friction is decreased by social trade.

Social commerce systems shorten the number of steps between discovery and purchase, which lowers friction and streamlines the purchasing process. Simple usability promotes impulsive purchasing, which raises conversion rates.

seamless and practical shopping experience.

Customers find social commerce to be a very easy alternative because of in-app checkout and preserved payment details. This hassle-free experience appeals particularly to a market where transactions are swift and simple.

Experiences with frictionless purchasing can boost client loyalty.

Social commerce enables transactions and fosters customer loyalty through its expedited purchasing procedure. Long-term client relationships and recurring business are fostered by a seamless experience.

3. Credibility based on peer endorsement.

more evaluations and suggestions as a result of social proof.

Social evidence, such as evaluations and recommendations, can be created and shown through social commerce platforms, influencing the decisions of prospective customers.

User-generated material to increase consumer trust

Consumer trust is bolstered by the incorporation of user-generated content (UGC) into social commerce platforms, such as comments and shares. Social evidence is a potent recommendation that increases trust in judgments made about purchases.

4. A rise in sales.

increasing conventional eCommerce's revenue

Forecasts indicate a large surge in sales through these channels, demonstrating the huge revenue driving power of social commerce. Because of its ease of use and integration, social commerce presents a lucrative alternative to conventional e-commerce tactics.

You have access to a very specific market to sell to.

Brands are able to precisely target their advertising and present products to people who are most likely to be interested because of the abundance of data about social media users. This focused strategy works well for social commerce, increasing sales and engagement, but it is difficult to duplicate in standard eCommerce sales environments.

Implementing Effective Social Commerce Strategies:

To capitalize on social commerce in 2024, businesses must implement strategies that are consistent with modern consumers' preferences and behaviors.

Here are a few proven ways to strengthen your social ecommerce strategies:Be true to yourself and your brand identity.

Connecting with your customers is the first step in reinforcing your ecommerce business's social media strategy. You can accomplish this by showcasing some brand personality. You may consider how to showcase the brand's personality. Social media is the ideal toolkit for developing an engaging brand personality. Use humor to make it more appealing. Remember that your goal is to engage your target audience in a meaningful way. Your brand personality is the foundation for doing it efficiently.

For example, if your brand is committed to sustainability, you can provide regular updates on eco-friendly initiatives. This encourages followers to make small changes in their daily lives.

Influencer Marketing

By 2024, the influencer landscape has moved beyond sponsored posts. Businesses are now collaborating with influencers to create authentic and engaging content that connects with their target audience. Authenticity is essential, and consumers are more likely to trust recommendations from influencers who actually use and believe in the products they promote. Micro-influencers have grown in popularity due to their niche audiences, allowing businesses to effectively connect with specific demographics.

AI-powered personalization:

Artificial intelligence (AI) is revolutionizing social commerce by allowing businesses to provide highly personalized experiences. In 2024, AI algorithms will analyze user behavior, preferences, and previous purchases to recommend products tailored to specific customers. This level of personalization not only improves the customer's shopping experience, but it also increases the chances of conversion by presenting them with products that match their preferences.

Incorporate Videos.

According to a study, 88% of people want brands to provide more video-based interactive content. It educates the audience about the services/products that the brands provide. When posting content on social media, you should make the most of the power of videos. It will allow you to better showcase your brand's personality. Make sure you've included high-quality video with relevant information about your product/service.

For example, you can use video Instagram stories to promote products or share brand stories. This will help to create a more engaging experience.

Shoppable Content: Adding shopping features to social media content has revolutionized social commerce. Businesses can now tag products in their posts on platforms such as Instagram and Facebook, allowing users to easily discover and purchase items. Furthermore, short-form videos like TikTok and Instagram Reels have become popular channels for shoppable content, allowing businesses to showcase products in a fun and engaging way.

Post user-generated content: In today's competitive market, unique and interactive content can help a brand stand out. On that note, user-generated content plays an important role in increasing brand advocacy. You can add user-generated content to your social media content calendar. This type of content may include product unboxing, user reviews, or feedback from a customer who has used an item.

Encourage your customers to provide valuable feedback via photos or videos. Once they've shared the content, you can reshare it from your company page. This increases engagement, and customers will feel connected to your brand.

Use Social Listening: When you prioritize your social media ecommerce strategy over social attention, you miss out on something. Using social listening, you can identify your competitor's strategic gaps. You can also find out what the industry is talking about. These insights will be used to create new products and marketing strategies that better meet the needs of the target audience.

Use a combination of paid and organic strategies: The most effective way to strengthen your social media ecommerce strategy is to use a combination of paid and organic strategies. Paid social media allows you to reach a larger audience, whereas organic content keeps them coming back.

Here are some mixed strategies-

- Increase brand visibility by using relevant hashtags.
- Boost posts and run paid advertisements.
- Use user-generated content for social proof.

- Launch influencer marketing campaigns.
- Establish brand partnerships.
- Ensure exceptional customer service for your social media ecommerce business.

Post consistently: Regular posting will help you stay in touch with your customers. Moving forward, it will help you gain traction through your marketing strategy. A regular posting schedule with a variety of content will help you stay afloat in this competitive market.

Offer exclusive promotions: Use various social media handles to provide your followers with exclusive promotions and exciting discounts. This will encourage them to make a purchase and foster greater customer loyalty. For example, if you sell teen t-shirts, you can give a 30% discount on certain products for a limited time. This would create a sense of urgency among followers to purchase the product at a discounted price.

3 Top Social Media Ecommerce Tools for 2024

Do you feel stuck despite using the best social media ecommerce strategies? That can happen at any time if you do not have the necessary tools. Here are the three best tools for your next strategy:

1. VidyBack

VidyBack uses real-time data to create engaging videos for your brand. The automation algorithm powers this tool's operation, allowing you to promote products/services to your target audience at the right time. This completely free app takes a few minutes to understand your company. Based on this, it generates appealing videos that you can share immediately. However, PRO features are also available to unlock some unique items.

2) Hootsuite

This social media management tool allows your brand to manage multiple social media accounts from one place. It also provides ecommerce integration, allowing you to sell your products directly through social media channels. You can monitor social media performance while improving your sales strategy.

3) Shopify

One of the well-known ecommerce platforms that allows you to sell your services/products through social media. Like Hootsuite, it provides social media integration as well as other features such as order fulfillment, inventory management, and payment processing.

Challenges and Considerations for E-Commerce Founders

Navigating algorithmic changes

Social media is constantly changing. Today's trending post could become tomorrow's digital ghost. Founders must remain agile, keeping up with platform changes and adjusting strategies to ensure consistent visibility.

Maintaining Brand Authenticity

Maintaining a genuine brand voice on commercial platforms can be challenging. It's a delicate balance between promotion and connection, selling a product versus selling a vision.

Platform diversification

Relying on a single platform is a risky game. Founders must create a cohesive multi-platform narrative that maintains brand consistency while leveraging each platform's unique strengths. For example, TikTok's partnership with Shopify enables merchants to reach a younger audience, whereas Snapchat's Shoppable AR offers an interactive shopping experience. Diversifying across these platforms can provide a wider reach and more engaging opportunities.

Conclusion

To begin, the power of Artificial Intelligence (AI) in personalization in 2024 has skyrocketed. AI systems can now evaluate user behavior with high accuracy, allowing marketers to provide individualized content to each individual. The figures are remarkable, with organizations who have implemented advanced personalization strategies reporting an incredible return on investment of $20 for every $1.

Consider chatbots that respond instantly, learn client preferences, and direct them to suitable items or services. Consider recommendation engines, which recommend products based on a user's browsing history and purchasing patterns, making the shopping experience more personal.

Personalization in 2024 will entail more than simply mentioning a customer's first name in an email; it will also require a thorough understanding of their wants and desires.

Second, if you haven't seen it already, authenticity, connection, and human involvement are emerging as critical audience requirements for brand interactions in 2024. Who better to promote a product than a reliable friend or neighbor? Celebrity endorsements have lost traction, so employ "nano influencers" and user-generated content to promote your company.

The CPG brand successfully places its products in the context of real-life households throughout the continent, building trust and relevance with their key customers.

The dominance of video content in marketing opens up several opportunities for firms. Meanwhile, building a small, focused creative team helps ensure the production of high-quality content that appeals to your target audience. As a result, small businesses should embrace the video content trend and invest in forming a dynamic creative team to optimize their marketing potential.

Furthermore, building a dedicated social media community is more than a short-term goal; it is a strategic long-term investment that will pay off handsomely in the near future. A thriving and active community can propel your business to success, give your followers a sense of belonging, and convert passive onlookers into enthusiastic brand champions.

Building a dedicated social media network is a strategic long-term investment that will yield considerable benefits in the near future.

However, when developing this community, it is vital to understand the dynamics of several platforms and avoid placing all of your eggs in one basket. As we noted in our informative post, Why We Don't Place Too Much Trust in Referrals in Facebook Groups, relying entirely on one sort of engagement or platform might be constraining. Instead, we urge that you diversify your social media strategy.

This means not just fostering open dialogue and promoting user-generated material, but also ensuring that your efforts are spread over numerous platforms and mediums in order to establish a strong and enduring online presence.

Finally, social commerce has advanced significantly since its inception, from basic integrations to complex, immersive shopping experiences. In 2024, social commerce is defined by seamless integration across several platforms, allowing firms to interact with customers in real time and offer a personalized buying experience. It's all about providing rich and interactive purchasing experiences.

AR is an effective tool for creating new and engaging social media marketing campaigns. Businesses may use augmented reality to captivate attention, promote engagement, and increase brand awareness. This increased degree of interaction not only improves the customer experience, but it also lowers the likelihood of returns.

As we embrace the prospects given by social commerce in 2024, it becomes evident that integrating social media and e-commerce is no longer an option for firms looking to remain competitive. Businesses can fully capitalize on the potential of social commerce to increase sales and create long-term consumer connections by taking a multi-platform approach, creating immersive shopping experiences, and executing effective methods. As technology advances, remaining adaptable and adjusting to changing consumer preferences will be critical to success in the dynamic world of social commerce.

Understanding and adopting these trends into your content strategy can help you catch attention, drive sharing, and establish deeper connections with your target audience in today's ever-changing social media environment.

Implementing the tactics and insights mentioned in this article can help you connect with your audience on a deeper level, enhance engagement, and meet your marketing goals. Accept the future of social media marketing, and you'll see that the opportunities are limitless.

As you plan for these exciting new advances in social media marketing in 2024, remember that the road to digital success is never-ending and ever-changing. If you're ready to fully realize the potential of these cutting-edge tactics but don't know where to start, we can help.

www.ingramcontent.com/pod-product-compliance
Lightning Source LLC
Chambersburg PA
CBHW052155220526
45471CB00004B/1696